EXPLORING
WITH THE MICROSCOPE

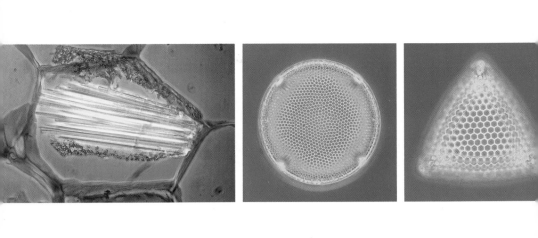

EXPLORING
WITH THE
MICROSCOPE

A BOOK OF DISCOVERY &LEARNING

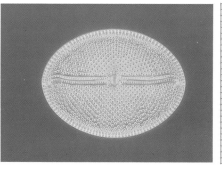

Werner Nachtigall

Sterling Publishing Co., Inc.
New York

Translated by Elizabeth Reinersmann

English translation edited by Isabel Stein, with assistance from the author and Dr. David Miyamoto, Department of Biology, Drew University, Madison, New Jersey, and Dorothy Suecoff, Department of Biology, Stuyvesant High School, New York, New York, whose invaluable help is gratefully acknowledged

Library of Congress Cataloging-in-Publication Data

Nachtigall, Werner.
    [Mikroskopieren. English]
    Exploring with the microscope : a book of discovery & learning /
    Werner Nachtigall.
       p.   cm.
    Includes index.
    ISBN 0-8069-0866-1
    1. Microscopes—Juvenile literature. 2. Microscopy—Juvenile
    literature. [1. Microscopes. 2. Microscopy.] I. Title.
    QH278.N3313   1995
    578—dc20   94-23844
                                                        CIP
                                                        AC

10 9 8 7 6 5 4 3 2 1

First paperback edition published in 1996 by
Sterling Publishing Company, Inc.
387 Park Avenue South, New York, N.Y. 10016
Originally published by BLV Verlagsgesellschaft mbH
under the title *Mikroskopieren: Geräte, Objekte, Praxis*
© 1994 by BLV Verlagsgesellschaft mbH, München, Germany
English translation © 1995 by Sterling Publishing Co., Inc.
Distributed in Canada by Sterling Publishing
℅ Canadian Manda Group, One Atlantic Avenue, Suite 105
Toronto, Ontario, Canada M6K 3E7
Distributed in Great Britain and Europe by Cassell PLC
Wellington House, 125 Strand, London WC2R 0BB, England
Distributed in Australia by Capricorn Link (Australia) Pty Ltd.
P.O. Box 6651, Baulkham Hills, Business Centre, NSW 2153, Australia
Printed and bound in Hong Kong
All rights reserved

Sterling ISBN 0-8069-0866-1 Trade
              0-8069-0867-X Paper

PREFACE

Everybody has a secret love and mine—among others—is the hidden world of microscopy. As a biologist I work with beautifully designed, specialized microscopes made by well-known manufacturers. At home, however, my favorite microscope is the classic binocular compound microscope. Even when I was a youngster, and later a student, I always had microscopes, some courageously made from old, hand-me-down lenses, empty pill containers, which served as tubes, and scraps of plywood. So, I know what it means to improvise and what it is like to have a great deal of enthusiasm and no money. Precisely for this reason I am going to share with you in this book many different methods and tricks that cost little or nothing at all.

I have also asked myself if the word "hobby" has to be synonymous with "cheap," however. Somebody who pursues hunting as a hobby does not need a muzzle-loader and neither does he use a cheap pair of binoculars; a motorcyclist might spend a goodly sum for her machine: in other words, we are willing to spend money on our hobbies. Why then shouldn't the amateur microscopist look for solid equipment like that used in research? For this reason, we will also take a look at the equipment and procedures used by professionals.

Since this is meant to be a hands-on book and microscopes have to be purchased (after all, they don't come falling out of the sky), I have also included the names of a number of manufacturers. The list is not intended to favor them more than others; it is meant only as a guide for beginners in the initial search for the items they will need.

The first part of the book deals with the microscope, how to handle it, its design, and photomicrography. The second part discusses how to prepare a specimen, with special attention given to the process of examining botanical, zoological, and mineralogical specimens. The third part tells about the magical world hidden in a drop of pond water. All is designed on one hand to aid the amateur microscopist in getting to know the equipment in detail and, on the other hand, to show the many ways in which a microscope can be used.

The most beautiful description cannot replace the fascination that comes from actually working with a microscope, however. Of course, disappointments are part of the game and mistakes will happen. Most mistakes, although they are small ones, are usually the result of improper handling of the equipment. Less often, they are the result of improper handling of specimens. Many possible mistakes are discussed, which is helpful in learning the tricks you can use to avoid them. This increases the fun you will have when you begin your journey into the fascinating world of microscopy.

CONTENTS

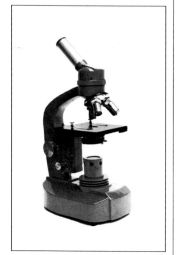

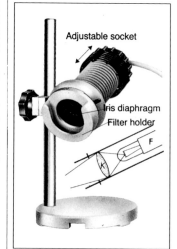

Adjustable socket

Iris diaphragm

Filter holder

F

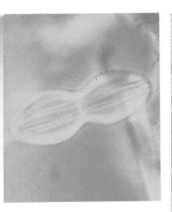

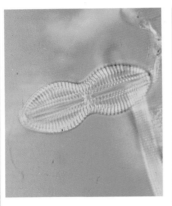

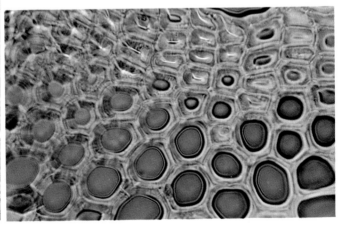

CONTENTS

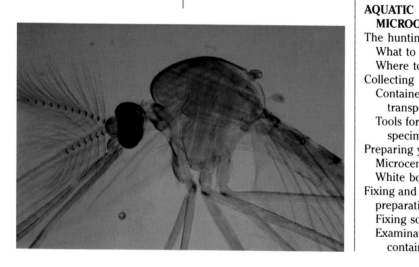

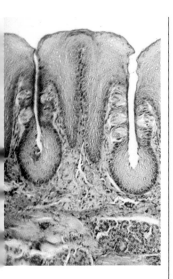

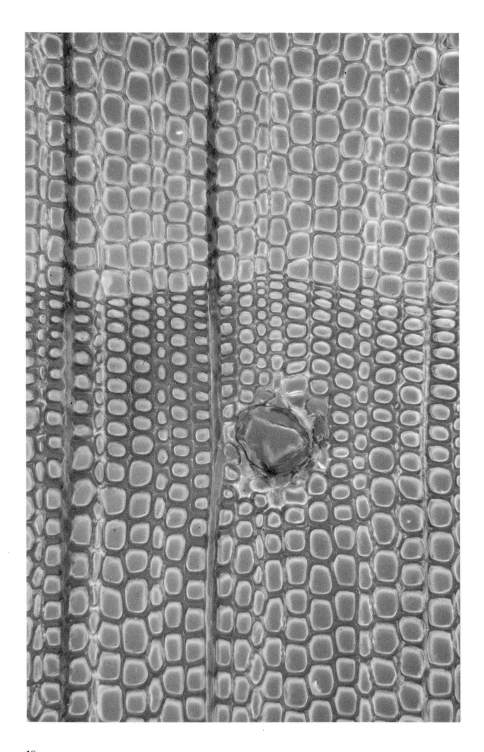

THE MICROSCOPE

Basic types

We distinguish between two basic types of microscope. In the standard microscope, the image-forming optics are above the stage, which is illuminated from below. In an inverted microscope, this arrangement is reversed and the specimen is illuminated from above. These inverted microscopes, though very expensive, are very practical for viewing objects like plankton in large containers. If you

Modern microscope designs. Left, a standard microscope; right, an inverted microscope.

don't want to specialize in such explorations, you will be quite satisfied with the standard microscope. Of course, now you have to make choices, and there are many. All manufacturers of course will swear that theirs is the best microscope. However, such assurances are not always

Cross-section of a piece of wood showing the border between annular rings.

correct. Microscopes from well-known manufacturers are usually good, and some are excellent. But often microscopes from a less-well-known manufacturer can compete quite successfully with better-known brand names, and they are usually much less expensive. Do a lot of comparison shopping if you have to be careful about your expenses.

Almost every manufacturer offers a variety of microscopes, from beginner models to those that you build up over time. Let's first concentrate on the less complicated and the least expensive ones.

What to buy in the beginning

I venture to say that this question is almost irrelevant, because no well-known manufacturers will sell microscopes that either have poor mechanics or poor optics. Even those offered in department stores are often quite solid. When looking at the basic microscopes that are available on the market (often called, undeservedly, "student models") you will find that they differ widely in design, in the extras they offer, and in their prices. All you can do is compare, always keeping in mind that changes are being made all the time, not only in what particular manufacturers offer but also in the prices they charge. I have included in the appendix names and addresses of the many well-

known companies. The best advice I can give to interested people is to write to *every* company and ask for their catalog; they will send it gladly. After all, everyone is looking for potential customers.

Should I buy an inexpensive microscope?

A word about the toy microscopes available in general stores (not specialty stores), which are often inexpensive. They are sold in fancy boxes filled with all kinds of nonessential odds and ends. All too often—believe me—these odds and ends are only good for the wastebasket. Don't waste your time buying such a microscope; all you will do is spoil the fun that is in store for you when you begin your hobby.

Of course, you will find small microscopes that can be expanded. If it does not bother you that they are not sturdy, you can, nevertheless, work with them quite adequately. However, make sure that you are able to connect standard objectives to the model you buy (see page 28). I also would recommend highly that a condenser with an iris diaphragm can be connected to the microscope (see page 44) and that there be a place for plugging in a light (see page 43).

The parts of the microscope

Every microscope is an optical instrument that consists of several mechanical and optical parts. Using the Olympus CH microscope as an example, let's look at these parts. The microscope stand has a base (B), which is often equipped with an illuminator. The stage (S) is attached to the stand with a mechanism for height adjustment. Usually a mechanical stage (MS), a device that moves the specimen around, is attached to the stage. On the underside is the *condenser holder (CH)*, which is also adjustable (and preferably has a mechanism to center the condenser. Above the stage is the *revolving nosepiece*, to which the objectives are attached. Above that is the *tube* with the *eyepiece(s)* or *ocular(s)*.

The microscope, as it appears in this drawing, has an illuminator with a *light source* within the optical axis. *Collector lenses* (similar to those in cameras) in the vicinity of the *illuminated field diaphragm* (a diaphragm whose image delimits the illuminated field in the object) produce an almost parallel ray bundle of light. This ray bundle is collected by the condenser (usually a double-lens condenser with an additional iris diaphragm below, the so-called *condenser diaphragm* or *aperture diaphragm*), and centered on the *object* (specimen). The object is illuminated by transmitted light. Such an object may be contained, for instance, in a drop of water on the *microscope slide*, a standardized glass slide that is placed on the stage and covered with an extremely thin *cover glass (cover slip)*. The light beam, diverging after it has passed through the specimen, is now collected by an *objective* and, being bent at an angle via a prism, is guided into the *eyepiece* or *ocular*. The light ray emerging from the eyepiece now meets the retina of the viewer's eye. The eye, therefore, is an integral part of the optical system of the microscope.

With a binocular microscope, both eyes are used for observation, which is much less fatiguing than using just one eye. If it is at all possible from a financial point of view, consider purchasing a binocular microscope. Your eyes will thank you, particularly if you intend to use your microscope a great deal.

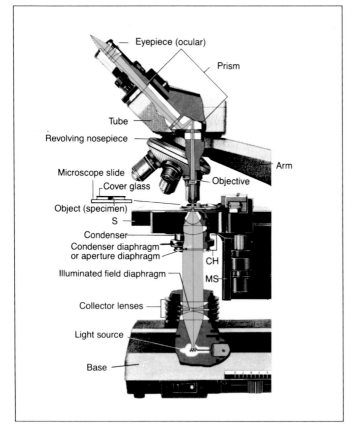

Eyepiece (ocular)
Prism
Tube
Revolving nosepiece
Microscope slide
Cover glass
Object (specimen)
S
Condenser
Condenser diaphragm or aperture diaphragm
Illuminated field diaphragm
Collector lenses
Light source
Base
Arm
Objective
CH
MS

Parts of a microscope and the path of transmitted light, shown on the Olympus CH (see text for details).

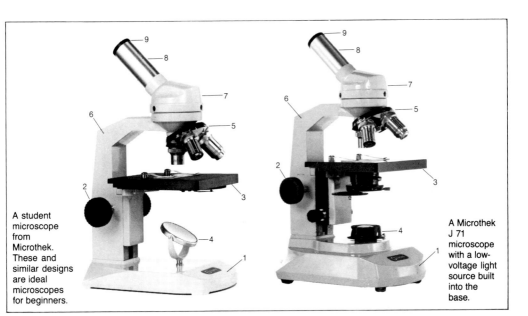

A student microscope from Microthek. These and similar designs are ideal microscopes for beginners.

A Microthek J 71 microscope with a low-voltage light source built into the base.

What should you expect from a hobby microscope?

In my opinion, it should have the features shown in the above photos, namely (numbers correspond to photos):

1. A stable base.

2. Finely calibrated mechanism that focuses the object by lowering and raising the stage. Adjustment knobs that focus by raising the tube and objectives will become annoying as soon as a camera is attached to the microscope; the added weight will "push the object out of focus."

3. A sufficiently large microscope stage with slide-holding clips that can be removed and, possibly, with predrilled holes for an attachable mechanical stage

to be added later. The stage should, at the very least, be equipped with a condenser sleeve, or, even better, a rack-and-pinion arrangement underneath for later installation of a substage condenser. The condenser should have an iris diaphragm and a swing-out filter holder; an auxiliary lens that can be swung out to illuminate the field of view, particularly when using low-power magnification, is also useful.

4. A flat mirror that is easy to remove and easy to replace with an inexpensive plug-in illuminator; even better, an integrated low-voltage illuminator, which is increasingly becoming standard on more and more models, even the very smallest.

5. A revolving triple nosepiece with standardized high-quality threads that will accommodate objectives of 160-mm tube length and 45-mm parfocalizing distance, if possible.

With such provisions in place, one can add lens systems from anywhere in the world—a possibility not to be underestimated. As far as objectives are concerned, in the beginning an inexpensive achromat will do quite well; however, you might want to think about buying instead a slightly more expensive semi-apochromat (see page 29). Whatever you decide, make sure that you have low-power magnifying lenses, e.g., $4 \times$, $10 \times$, and $20 \times$. The highest magnification for a dry objective usually is $40 \times$. If you are thinking anyway of adding such an objective in the future, consider buying a 4-objective nosepiece that allows you to attach, for instance, 4×, 10×, 20×, and 40× objectives.

Condenser with filter holder and swing-in condenser lens.

Rotatable stage with slide.

Plug-in low-voltage lamp.

High-magnification objectives should be spring-loaded in order to avoid accidental breakage of the cover slip and damage to the front lens.

6. A stable stand that allows the user to safely lift the microscope off the table.

7. A monocular, *removable* tube that can be rotated.

Being able to remove and exchange tubes is important for, as the saying goes, "appetite grows with the eating." Those whose interest is in research will, sooner or later, want to have a binocular microscope, and those who want to specialize in photomicrography should be looking at trinocular tubes or a (much less expensive) monocular photo tube. The latter easily attaches to standard ring dovetails.

8. Inclined tubes for comfortable viewing; they reduce eyestrain and tension of the neck muscles, something that should be taken into consideration even when buying a monocular microscope.

9. An eyepiece that gives you low to medium magnifica-

Nosepiece for 4 objectives.

tion (6× to 10×) with standard outer diameter of 23.2 mm.

Standardized eyepieces can be combined with optical accessories from manufacturers from all over the world without difficulty, which is an advantage. If they are not standardized you can use only those eyepiece–objective combinations that fit your particular microscope (see page 33).

To summarize the above: even the smallest "beginner's microscope" should include the following: A heavy body with a sound focusing mechanism; standard objectives and standard eyepieces, mounted at an angle; a revolving nosepiece; an illumination device; and condensers and tubes that can be changed.

Such a microscope will serve you well in the beginning. If you have the means to add a few components, you will have a well-functioning research microscope. If you know from the outset that you eventually want to pursue serious research, do not make the mistake of starting too small, however. If you do, you might discover later that the student microscope you bought does not allow you to exchange the stage of the microscope for a rotating or mechanical stage, or that you won't be able to attach a low-voltage lamp—something you need for Köhler illumination (see page 46).

If you need a serious research microscope with the basic accessories in place, you must dig a little deeper into your pocket. If you spend more, you can buy a microscope of the type in the photo at the right, with similar components. It will satisfy the basic requirements, and additional components can easily be added on—for instance, those that allow you to do phase-contrast microscopy (see page 36).

What kind of optical components should a beginner buy?

Whatever you do, do not buy components that are not internationally standardized. Objectives must have standard threads (measured with a vernier calipers, the outer diameter should be 20 mm), and eyepieces with a standard diameter of 23.2 mm. As far as objectives are concerned, I would recommend in the beginning good-quality achromats, approximately $3\times$, $10\times$, and $20\times$ (possibly $40\times$), with simple Huygenian eyepieces between $6\times$ and $10\times$. A few tips when purchasing objectives:

- Whenever new models come out, manufacturers always have an ample supply of discontinued models on hand, and those left over are offered at surprisingly low prices; call or write to companies and ask for information.
- Some companies specialize in affordable single objectives because they have purchased "leftover" series from manufacturers.
- Last, but not least, some microscopists update their

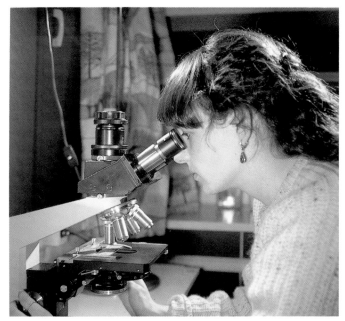

A solid basic piece of equipment (here a PZO microscope) has standard equipment that you will enjoy using for the rest of your life, to which objectives or photographic accessories can be added at any time. This particular microscope is equipped with a trinocular tube, for binocular viewing plus a tube to accommodate a camera.

equipment (they must have the latest) and are more than happy to sell the parts that they are replacing to a young colleague, often at a very reasonable price. After all, everybody was young at one time with plenty of enthusiasm but very little money. An advertisement in the newspaper is the best way to reach such persons.

A specialized or basic microscope?

To start with a very basic microscope and add accessories as you go along, or to buy a specially equipped microscope: that is the question. And it is very much a matter of

attitude—or better yet, of temperament. If you are very sure from the very beginning what you want to do with your microscope (and what you don't want to do), and if you already know that certain changeable accessories are of no interest to you, you may be able to have a supplier assemble a microscope to your exact specifications. The photos on page 16 show a typical series of such microscopes. The Swift 11TC is a basic elementary school microscope with widefield eyepiece; 4X, 10X, and 40X objectives; 5-aperture disc diaphragm; rack-and-pinion focus control; inclined observation tube; and mirror. A

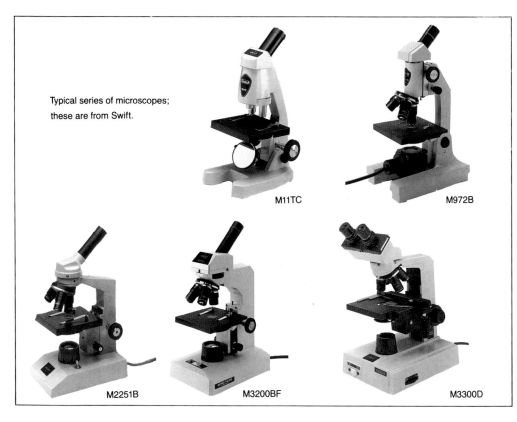

Typical series of microscopes; these are from Swift.

M11TC

M972B

M2251B

M3200BF

M3300D

plug-in illuminator may be added. The Swift M2251B has an inclined tube that is rotatable 360°; widefield eyepiece with built-in pointer; a built-in condenser and disk diaphragm with 5 apertures; and separate coarse and fine controls. The Swift M970 is an advanced student microscope with choice of widefield, Huygenian, or zoom eyepieces; either upright or inclined tube; retractable color-coded objectives; built-in condenser with adjustable diaphragm; choice of mirror or illuminator; rack-and-pinion coarse adjustment; and roller-type fine adjustment. The

Swift M3200BF series microscope has a built-in condenser with adjustable diaphragm; calibrated widefield eyepiece scale; tension control for sensitive focusing; built-in illuminator; and is available in monocular or binocular versions. The Swift M3300D series advanced microscope has, in addition, a focusable condenser; choice of built-in illuminators; and it can be used with an adapter and a 35-mm SLR camera.

The microscopes described above are meant as examples only; different models and

types are offered by other manufacturers.

Microscopes to which diverse accessories can be added over time are something else altogether. As an example, see the photo on page 17; every large company offers similar models. If desired, all kinds of accessories can be added on and around the stand of such a microscope, shown here with an adjustable halogen lamp. A polarizing filter can be added to the light aperture (see page 35). Either a standard or a mechanical stage can be added to the arm. The condenser holder will accept standard or phase-contrast condensers, the latter individually (one for each objective) or in a rotating turret. The rotatable nosepiece can hold either 3, 4, or 5 objectives. The viewing tube, shown here as a trinocular tube that accepts either a 35-mm or an instant camera (Polaroid), also accommodates a polarizing filter (analyzer; see page 35) or a Bertrand lens, which permits viewing of the objective's rear focal plane. An incident or fluorescent light illuminator also can be added between the Bertrand lens and the polarizing filter; this allows the operator to illuminate and observe the specimen from above.

The extreme versatility of such a microscope is sure to fascinate almost every microscopist. However, even if money is no object (and the cost of additional accessories I

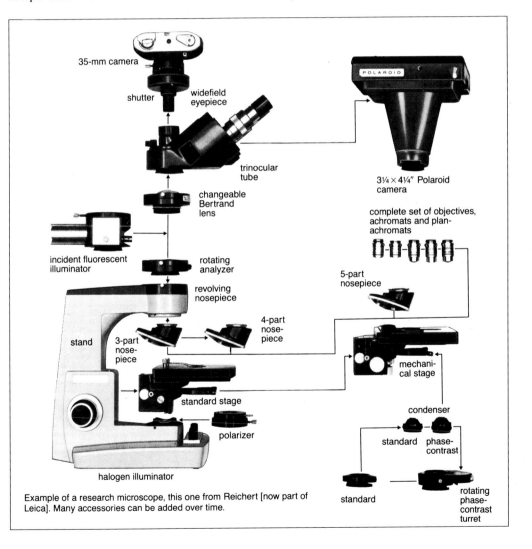

Example of a research microscope, this one from Reichert [now part of Leica]. Many accessories can be added over time.

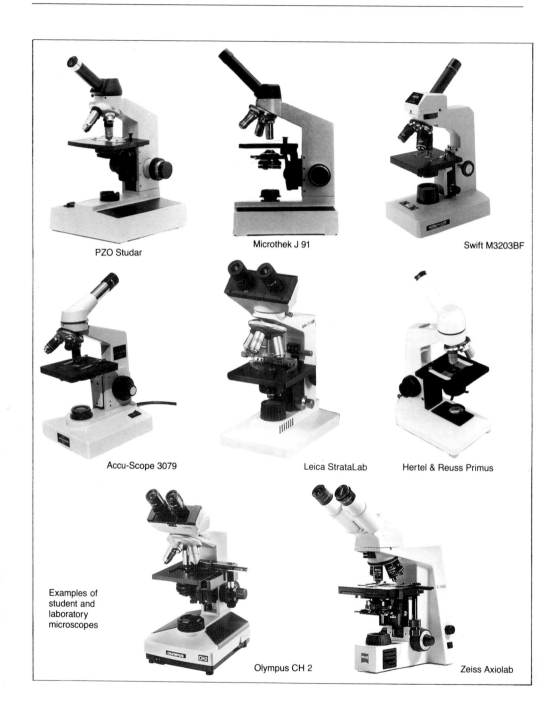

PZO Studar

Microthek J 91

Swift M3203BF

Accu-Scope 3079

Leica StrataLab

Hertel & Reuss Primus

Examples of
student and
laboratory
microscopes

Olympus CH 2

Zeiss Axiolab

have listed can be several times higher than that of the basic instrument), such a microscope has disadvantages as well as advantages. It takes time to change accessories and make the necessary calibrations. More times than not, I never get to do all the experiments I originally intended to do, because I just did not want to bother making the changes.

The all-around instrument for everyday work, like the ones we have discussed, usually includes only those combinations of accessories that can be mounted permanently and used over and over again. Now, of course, we are looking again at a special-purpose (but less expensive) model that you could have bought right from the start. But who can look into the future?

If you want to keep all your options open, start with a very basic, modern microscope, adding accessories as you go. The most important thing to keep in mind is that the "building blocks" you plan to add on should be interchangeable—even those that you are going to buy in the future. Microscopes built by world-renowned companies and designed for expansion are much different than they used to be in the past. The material used for the stands is die-cast aluminum and it has an opening to accommodate a light source. Various mechanical systems that focus the lenses and adjust the position of stage and condenser are built into the stand. Various tubes, nosepieces, stages, and condenser turrets can be mounted to couplings on the stand and held in place by tightening screws.

The student microscope

The more basic instruments, which dispense with fancy and expensive refinements, are known as *student microscopes*. However, the name is deceiving. Even though these instruments are primarily found in schools, they are not restricted to that use alone. On the contrary; these are the perfect microscopes for the beginning hobbyist! They are by no means "cheap" instruments— either literally or figuratively. There are reasons why the buyer of such a microscope won't be disappointed, discussed below.

All eight microscopes shown on the opposite page have standard optics and provide the minimum requirements for a microscope to which other accessories can be added in the future, as we have already discussed. Such classic models have been available for some time. However, the market is changing fast; some models have undergone changes and new instruments are being developed all the time. With a little bit of luck one can find discontinued models that are much less expensive. Like everything else, microscopes are also subject to trends, and it is not necessary to insist on the newest design. As already suggested, write to distributors or manufacturers and ask for information.

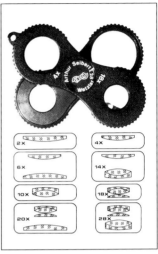

Various possible lens combinations with a hand-held multiple-lens magnifier from EMO.

Hand-held microscopes and magnifying glasses

I do not recommend hand-held microscopes. They are difficult to handle, often have poor light sources (even though a few come with a built-in lamp), and usually have poor resolution. On the other hand, hand-held magnifying glasses mounted in a protective sleeve are often very useful for a preliminary examination of a specimen. Lenses that have a light source with a built-in battery are also very handy. A very comfortable magnifying instrument is the Octoskop (from Emo/Wetzlar), which has a combination of 4 lenses with 8 different magnifications. A machinist's 3-lens folding pocket magnifier from Edmund Scientific is a similar magnifier.

The Swift FM31 field microscope.

Pocket and field microscopes

I am continually amazed at the number of small instruments that practically fit into the pocket of one's trousers and are therefore easily taken on a trip. They are only suitable for preliminary examinations, however. In the 1980s, an inverted field microscope was manufactured by Swift. It produces astounding resolution. It is an unusual microscope that features standard eyepieces and a three-part rotatable nosepiece; however, limited space precluded use of standard objectives. It is no longer manufactured; however, another field microscope, the FM31, is currently made by Swift. It weighs 2 lbs. and is equipped with a battery-powered incandescent lamp and 3 objectives.

For preliminary examination, I have an entirely different and extremely inexpensive solution. Buy a very cheap department-store microscope and replace the objective with a simple standard achromatic 10× lens. A mechanic will

make you a threaded adapter. Usually the eyepieces are not all that bad and the weakest one can often be used. The only thing you must make sure of is that the height of the drive can be adjusted far enough, because the standard objectives are longer than the small built-in objectives; if necessary, the rotatable nosepiece has to be removed.

Stereomicroscopes

Many well-known manufacturers have developed beauti-

Through a binocular microscope, the internal structure of the stem of a stinging nettle (Urtica dioica), with its stinging hairs, is particularly easy to view using incident illumination. In this photo you can see the stem in its natural colors.

ful, and very expensive, stereomicroscopes with sufficient room to accommodate larger specimens and zoom lenses with magnification anywhere between 4× and 40×, as well as incident and transmitted illumination. In other words, they come with everything that your heart could desire. Since each eye views the object from a slightly different angle, a remarkable 3-dimensional effect is achieved. Such microscopes are very useful even for the beginner; for instance, when selecting a plankton from a Petri dish, when viewing an insect, looking at mosses, and so forth. Many less-well-known manufacturers have brought stereomicroscopes on the market that are surprisingly inexpen-

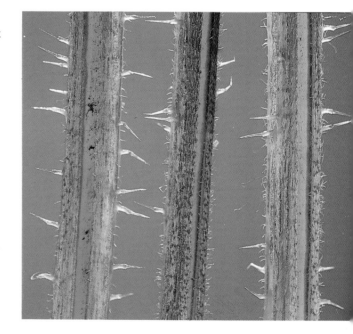

sive and are equipped with very adequate lenses. Allowances have to be made for the mechanics, the ease of usage, and the exchangeable lenses.

When you buy inexpensive stereomicroscopes, you will find that very often the images both eyes see do not match and that your eyes are getting tired rather quickly. The cause is less a matter of poor lenses than a matter of insufficient adjustment, which you will have do yourself. First make sure that the prisms are securely fastened—often the screws are loose. The objectives are in eccentric, turnable, and movable aluminum tubes, and are fastened on the sides with small screws. Loosen these screws on one side, push the objective tube into the instrument as far as it will go and turn it slowly around its long axis. While viewing a small, light object on a dark background, watch how the two images move about. Turn until the two images become one and the object appears to be three-dimensional. If you are unsuccessful, loosen the screw on the other tube, and turn both tubes slowly towards each other until you suddenly see one three-dimensional image. At that point, ask somebody to fasten the screws for you.

If you have a small pair of binoculars from Zeiss, look at the stand the company produces to turn these binoculars into a stereomicroscope. Both parts together make up a fine, handy binocular inspection microscope, but they are not inexpensive.

Here, again, I can only recommend: look at advertisements; put an advertisement in the paper yourself to find people who want to upgrade their existing model. It should be possible to buy a solid, older

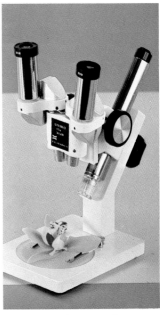

Small, inexpensive stereomicroscope from Eschenbach.

instrument for less than 20% of the price for a new, modern version.

OPTICS

Cost-performance ratio

The objective is the soul of the microscope. It produces the all-important intermediate image within the tube, which the eyepiece only magnifies. If the intermediate image is poor, the subsequent magnified image is even worse. A combination of poor illumination and wrong objective will render even the best microscope useless, and vice versa; a simple instrument can produce an astounding improvement in resolution if a bad objective is exchanged for a good one and optimal illumination is provided.

The pictures on the top right and middle (the bases of hair roots from a mouse embryo) were taken with an inexpensive $20 \times$ objective. The photo on the right side (top row) was taken with the $10 \times$ eyepiece, with total magnification of $20 \times 10 = 200$ (see text on page 27) and a simple built-in bulb from a flashlight. The photo on the top left was taken with a zoom eyepiece at $20 \times$. The photo below it was taken with the same inexpensive objective that was mounted on a research microscope (with Köhler illumination and a good eyepiece). It is obvious that good illumination does

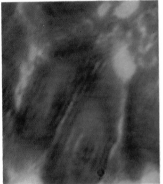
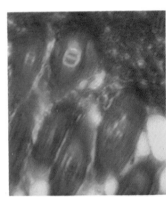
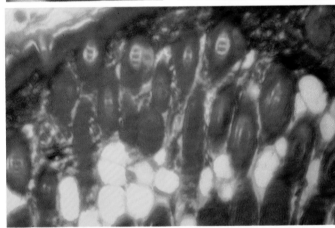
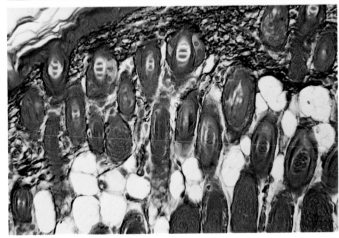

A set of modern objectives from Olympus.

Test photos taken with poor and good lenses (see text).

make a difference; however, resolution and sharpness are still not satisfactory.

The photo at the beginning of the chapter (page 22) shows a rotatable nosepiece with 5 modern objectives from Olympus. They are expensive. Objectives of similar quality from other world-renowned manufacturers are equal in price, like those from Leitz (now Leica) and Zeiss.

The photo at the bottom on page 23 was taken with a 20 × objective and an 8 × projection eyepiece from Olympus with optimal illumination (Köhler adjustment; compare page 46). Both resolution and sharpness are excellent.

Amateurs will find that the quality of their images are somewhere between the middle and the bottom photo. One can find very useful objectives—with 10 × to 40 × magnification—that will give life-long enjoyment and are unlikely to become outdated; these don't have to be very expensive. Conclusion: Above all, if you must economize, don't economize on lenses (in particular, on objectives) or illumination.

Some optical geometry

The path of a light ray

On pages 24 to 27, you will find a short course in optical geometry which, with the aid of the 12 consecutive drawings, will guide you from the very simple lens to a complete, assembled microscope. All those who are not interested in theory may, of course, skip this section. However, I don't think it would be wise. After all, a microscope, including the illumination, is a very complex optical system and one will be hard-pressed to make use of all the optical possibilities without knowing the principles behind them.

A convex lens (which is thicker at the center than at the edges) is a lens that allows parallel, incoming light rays (for example, sunlight) to be focused on one point (F) on the focal plane. (To simplify drawing the path of light, the lens can be represented in the drawing as a "substitute plane"; see Fig. 1.)

Since you can make light fall onto both sides of a lens (or a more complicated optical component) it must have two focal planes: a front focal plane P_f and a back focal plane P_b. The distances between each and the "substitute plane" are equal (Fig. 2).

The focal length (f) can be shortened by increasing the curvature of the lens, as well as by combining several converging lenses (Fig. 3). The path of the rays is reversible. If a point source of light (e.g., light bulb) is placed at the focal point (F), the light will exit the lens as parallel rays (Fig. 4).

These principles are used in the condenser.

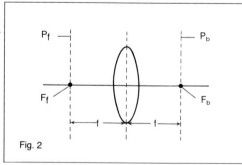

Fig. 2

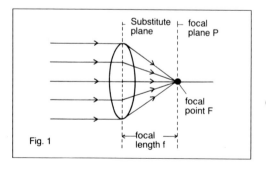

Substitute plane | focal plane P

focal point F

focal length f

Fig. 1

(This very important optical component is discussed in more detail on page 44). Light from a point source (e.g. a light bulb) leaves the collector lens in the base of the microscope as parallel rays. The diameter of this parallel beam of

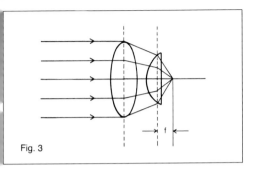

Fig. 3

light matches the diameter of the lower condenser lens (Fig. 5).

In a good illuminator, an adjustable iris diaphragm (field diaphragm) is placed close to the

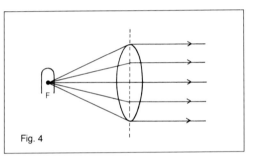

Fig. 4

base illuminator lenses. By opening or closing the field diaphragm, the diameter of the entering parallel beam can be controlled. Proper adjustment of both the field diaphragm and the aperture diaphragm in the condenser eliminates most of the peripheral rays that cause glare (Fig. 6). The vital importance of these two

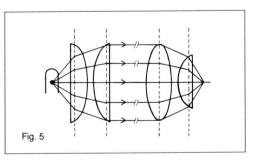

Fig. 5

diaphragms is discussed in more detail later (pages 45–47).

After the rays have passed through the focal

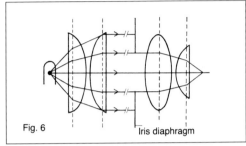

Fig. 6   Iris diaphragm

plane of the condenser, the rays will again diverge (Fig. 7). They are captured again by the front lens of the objective (Fig. 8).

The objective (here represented by its front lens only) produces a magnified and inverted

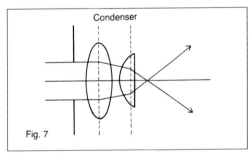

Condenser

Fig. 7

image of the object in the tube of the microscope. Imagine that our object is an arrow. We can draw three rays from the head of this arrow. A ray drawn from the head of the arrow

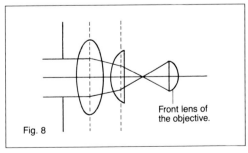

Fig. 8   Front lens of the objective.

25

through the front focal point (F_f) to the lens and out as a parallel ray is the *focal ray*. The *parallel ray* runs from the head of the arrow parallel to the optical axis, through the lens and back focal point (F_b). The *principal ray* runs directly from the head of the arrow to where the other two rays meet. Where the three rays intersect is where the intermediate image will be (Fig. 9).

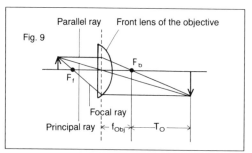

Fig. 9

The magnification of the objective V_{Obj} is the quotient of the optical tube length T_o and the focal length of the objective f_{Obj} (Fig. 9).

$$V_{Obj} = T_o/f_{Obj}.$$

With a small piece of ground glass held in the place where the image has been produced, you are able to "catch" this intermediate image. If the magnification is not sufficient, this image can be viewed with a magnifying glass.

Lens magnification
But how does a simple lens work? In order to understand its effect, you must consider the lens and the optics of the eye together.

You can see the image of an object clearly when the lens of the eye projects it directly onto the retina (Fig. 10). A person with normal

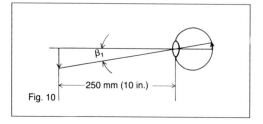

Fig. 10

eyesight can produce a sharply focused image of an object that is located 250 mm (10 in.) away from the eye (the "conventional viewing distance"). In the process the principal ray of the eye lens assumes a certain viewing angle β_1 to the visual axis of the eye. If you want the object to look larger, you must move closer to it. Here, however, the ability of the eye to focus is lost. You reach for a magnifying glass to help you out.

We may put the object in the front focal plane of the magnifying lens. As the drawing of the ray of the lens demonstrates, the image of the object that has been moved closer is now sharply focused on the retina and is also magnified: it appears on the eye over a wider viewing angle, β_2. If, for instance, the lens has a magnifying power of $5\times$, β_2 is also 5 times

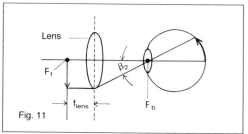

Fig. 11

larger than β_1 (Fig. 11).

We have gained two important insights. First: lens magnification really means that we are seeing the object at a wider viewing angle than we would if we viewed it with the naked eye at the conventional viewing distance of 250 mm (10 in.). Second: the amount of lens magnification V_{Lens} is calculated by the quotient of the "conventional viewing distance" and the focal length of the lens f_{Lens}, in other words: $V_{Lens} = 250\ mm/f_{Lens}$ (where f_{Lens} is also measured in millimeters).

The phenomenon of lens magnification is easily demonstrated as in the drawing below (p. 27): beside the parallel ray draw an additional ray and extend both away from the eye until they intersect. You now have created a "virtual image," which cannot be projected onto ground glass but that we also can see—or think we can see (see the drawing on page 27). In our example of a 5× lens, the virtual image of the arrow is also 5× as large as the arrow itself. With totally relaxed eyes (infinity corrected), the image itself is produced at infinity.

The compound microscope

The viewing lens in the drawing on page 26 is nothing else but an eyepiece, or more precisely, the eyelens of the eyepiece (the lens closest to the eye). The effect of a compound microscope can be summarized as follows: The objective magnification (V_{Obj}) produces a magnified, real intermediate image in the tube—that is, in the front focal plane (P_f) of the eyelens of the eyepiece [according to DIN standards, 10 mm (⅜ in.) below the upper end of the viewing tube]. This image is viewed via the lens of the eyepiece (magnification V_{OK}) and appears to us as a virtual image over a visual angle that is V_{Obj} times larger. (Since the round visual field diaphragm is in the same plane as that of the intermediate image, the image is sharp, too.) The *total magnification* of a microscope is equal to the product of the objective magnification V_{Obj} and the eyepiece magnification V_{OK}:

$$V_{microscope} = V_{Obj} \cdot V_{OK} = \frac{T_o}{f_{Obj}} \cdot \frac{250}{f_{OK}}$$

(all in mm; see Fig. 12). If the tube has additional lenses, you must multiply by the tube factor n_{tube}:

$$V_{microscope} = n_{tube} \cdot V_{Obj} \cdot V_{OK}$$

An objective with 10× magnification, an eyepiece with a 12× magnification, and a tube factor of 1.25 will give you $10 \cdot 12 \cdot 1.25 = 150×$ magnification.

For the purpose of describing the mechanical structure of a microscope, certain terminology has been established; for instance, "tube length" and "parfocalizing distance." In the past, these dimensions were often different for different manufacturers, which made it difficult to assemble optical parts from several countries. Today, manufacturers have standardized these dimensions. The mechanical tube length (the distance between the eyepiece-locating surface of the viewing tube and the objective-locating surface of the nosepiece) is 160 mm. The parfocalizing distance of the objective is 45 mm; this is the distance in air between the object plane (the uncovered surface of the object) and the objective-locating flange of the nosepiece. The parfocalizing distance of the eyepiece is 10 mm; it is the distance between the eyepiece-locating surface of the viewing tube and the primary image plane. These measurements are all DIN standard.

For the sake of completeness let me note that for approximately the last ten years, microscopes have been available that have been fitted with infinity-corrected objectives. Here it is possible to "catch" the path of the ray at any point, which has great advantages for laboratory work. For the hobby microscopist this is not all that important, unless he or she is a serious hobbyist and is thinking of buying a lot of accessories.

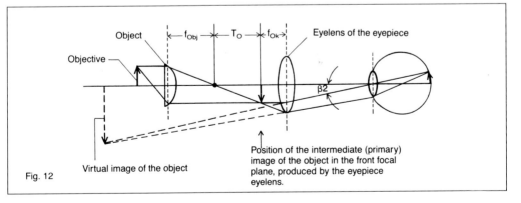

Fig. 12

Object f_{Obj} T_o f_{Ok} Eyelens of the eyepiece

Objective

β2

Virtual image of the object

Position of the intermediate (primary) image of the object in the front focal plane, produced by the eyepiece eyelens.

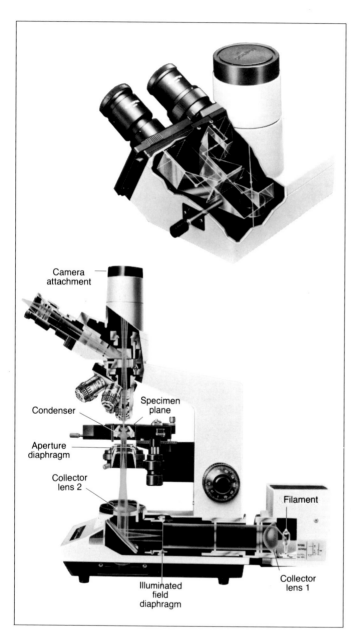

The path of a ray in a research microscope. (An illustration of the path of a ray with Köhler illumination can be found in the drawing on page 64.)

Objective basics

A good microscope objective is an optically and mechanically delicate masterpiece that is rather expensive. If you are interested in doing serious photomicrography, you should not look for less expensive ones. It is much better to economize when it comes to the base, camera, and accessories. The quality of your photographs is directly dependent on the quality of the objectives. If your finances are limited, I would recommend starting slowly; buy only one at a time. The first one might be a 20× objective, but buy one of exceptional quality. That is much better than buying a whole set of three or four objectives of varying magnifying power that are inferior.

A good objective should fulfill four requirements, discussed below.

1. It should have high resolving power, meaning that it should be able to produce clear images of structures within a specimen even when they are very close to each other.

The resolving power of a lens is determined by its *numerical aperture* (NA), the sine of ½ of the aperture angle β, multiplied by the refractive index (n) of the medium between the specimen and the objective: $NA = n \cdot \sin(\beta/2)$. The minimum resolvable distance d between two points is therefore:

$$d = \frac{\lambda}{2\,NA}$$

where λ = wavelength of light. This formula indicates that with shorter wavelength (bluish) light and with higher numerical aperture, the minimum resolvable distance becomes smaller, meaning the resolving power is increased. In addition:

2. The objective should clearly show points and not turn them into lines or curves.

3. A flat image should be projected flat.

4. Aberration due to different wavelengths of colored light should be kept to a minimum.

We know of no objective that is able to totally eliminate all optical aberrations. However, there are models on the market that have been able to a lesser or greater degree to minimize distortions. Standard, inexpensive *achromats* (achromatic objectives) have been corrected for the yellow–green part of the spectrum. Short wavelength colors (blue) and longer wavelength colors (like red) are not as well represented (causing tinted edges of the field).

A *plan-achromat* (or flat-field achromat) is an achromat that has been corrected more specifically for the curvature of the image field; this means that both the center *and* the edges of the specimen will be in sharp focus. *Semi-apochromats* or *fluorite systems* reduce tinted outer edges with the help of fluorite lenses. (These are also available in flat-field objectives.) *Apochromats* have been corrected for most chromatic aberra-

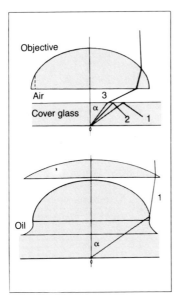

Main ray paths in a dry system (above) and an oil-immersion system (below). α = β/2, half the aperture angle.

tions. The remaining distortions that can't be eliminated are compensated for with special eyepieces. *Plan-apo-chromats* are apochromats that

An old, pre-WWII classic objective from Zeiss, and next to it a modern high-power objective.

have particularly flat field images.

As far as *immersion systems* are concerned, let me make some observations. *Dry systems* can only make use of a relatively small portion of a ray bundle (small numerical aperture, low resolving power) and from 40× and above magnification, they are dependent on an exact adherence to a very specific thickness of cover glass (see page 33). *Oil-immersion systems* use more of the ray bundle (rays 1 and 2 in the drawing at the left) and are not as dependent on the thickness of the cover glass. They have a higher numerical aperture and thereby higher resolving power, since the refractive index n of oil = 1.515; (n of air = 1.000). β of an oil system is higher than it is in the dry system. The immersion system has some drawbacks, however. For one thing, the working distance is very small (in the case of oil, with 100× magnification, usually less than 1/10 mm). This requires great care when focusing; specimens that are thicker often cannot be explored in greater depth. Also, one must clean the front lens with xylol (xylene) after each use. There are also *water immersion systems*, but these are very expensive.

Other important factors

The most important aspect of an objective is its ability to bring an image into as sharp focus as possible. However, we have a few other identifying

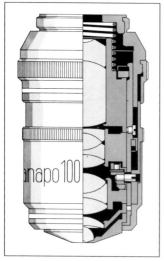

A cross-section of a world-class objective of the first order, a plan-apochromat 100/1.3 oil-immersion objective, made by Zeiss.

measurements that make working with objectives decidedly less complicated.

Standardization. As we have already mentioned, all objectives should be standardized (outer diameter, approximately 20 mm) and should be usable with a mechanical tube length of 160 mm. Their parfocalizing distance should be 45 mm. Attaching standard objectives to a revolving nosepiece gives you the assurance that the parfocalizing distance to the eyepiece is correct (if the tube length is 160 mm, the intermediate image is in the plane of the eyepiece image field diaphragm), which, in turn, means that the image will remain focused (approximately) when you change objectives. Bothersome refocusing thus is drastically reduced, or is not necessary at all.

Spring-Loaded Objectives. High-powered dry objectives ought to be spring-loaded. No matter how careful you are, it is inevitable that eventually you will lower an objective too far; those without spring-loading will then break the cover glass and you will scratch the front lens.

Centering the Rotatable Nosepiece. Nothing is more bothersome than when your object disappears from the field of view as you change to another objective. Good lenses and rotatable nosepieces are constructed in such a way that adequate centering will remain in place no matter what the magnification, even when you change to another objective. This should always be tested before you buy. However, you could calibrate your system yourself by adding thin paper rings and/or eccentrically clamping a section of such a ring between the *objective stop* and the *nosepiece opening*. However, this is a tricky process and requires a fair amount of patience on your part.

Increased Working Distance. On page 29 we gave an example of how minute the working distance is in high-power systems: only a fraction of a millimeter. However, in more recent designs one can achieve the same magnification with a significant increase in this distance (for instance, in the Olympus

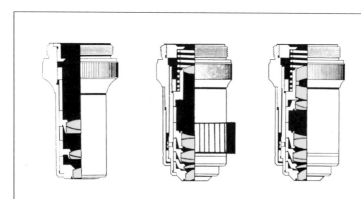

Cross sections of different types of objectives made by Meopta. From left to right: achromat; semi-apochromat; apochromat.
The objectives in the middle and on the right are spring-loaded, which serves to protect the cover glass from high pressure when it is accidentally hit. Note the different number and arrangement of the lenses.

Plan-objectives from the series NPL Fluotar, made by Leica (formerly Leitz). The markings on each are: magnification at the left of the slash mark, and numerical aperture to the right of the slash. The degree of magnification of each objective shown here increases by 1.6 over the weaker objective preceding it (from right to left in photo). This is a fluorite system of semi-apochromatic objectives; as far as the quality of correction is concerned, about halfway between the achromats and the apochromats.

LB objective; here the achromats have even more room than the apochromats). If you are able to invest some money in such a high-power dry system, you can buy yourself something that is much easier to handle.

Contrast. Multilens objectives tend to produce weak pictures because of the large number of reflecting surfaces. A particularly good contrast can be produced through geometrically optimizing the lenses (using high-power computers) and layering tricks (multiple compensation). This process has been achieved recently. It follows that modern objectives should be better (but aren't always) than those of the previous generations.

Objectives from pre-WWII microscopes that have not yet acquired the status of antiques (which are highly regarded by collectors and therefore are very expensive), and good objectives made after the war can often be purchased without much trouble and very reasonably through an ad in your daily paper or professional journal or magazine. The photo on the bottom of

page 32 was taken with such a 40x "classic." The black-and-white photos on pages 130 and 132 were also taken with such an objective.

Focusing on and examining a specimen

Focusing on the Object
Start out by adjusting the illumination (see page 46). Then, for low-, or medium-power objectives, lower the tube until the object comes into focus. With high-power objectives, the above procedure may lead to a broken cover glass and a scratched front lens if, as happens easily, you go beyond the focal point. It is better to proceed as follows: look at the tube from the side at an angle and lower it until the front lens of the objective almost touches the cover glass. Now look through the microscope and *raise* the tube until the image is in sharp focus.

Changing Objectives
Turn the rotatable nosepiece, preferably always in the same direction and always going from the lower to higher power, one notch at a time. If the objective is not securely set in the notch, the image will

be cut diagonally, with one side darker than the other. If the objectives are not properly focused, you run the danger of hitting the cover glass when moving to higher magnification. To avoid damaging the lens, do not use the coarse adjustment. It is better to slightly raise the tube first, and lower it again after the next objective is in place.

Centering an Object
Manual Adjustment without a Mechanical Stage. Support both hands by resting them either on the base or on the edge of the stage and carefully guide the slide with thumb and index finger. Since the moving image, unless you have compensating optics, is inverted and greatly magnified, it will be a bit difficult in the beginning to bring the specimen into the center of the field of view. But this will become easier with practice.

Mechanical Stage. By turning the control knobs, it is easy to move the slide gently in two perpendicular directions.
Rotating Stage. Except for unusual situations, a rotating stage works well for properly orienting a specimen in prepa-

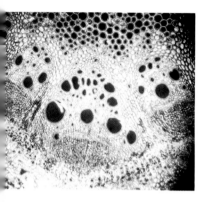

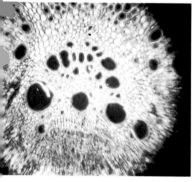

ration for photographing. However, you must be able to center the rotating stage.

Eyepieces (oculars)

As shown in the drawing on page 27, an eyepiece lets you see a magnified virtual image of the intermediate image produced by the objective. Such magnifying effect is accomplished by the eyelens of the eyepiece alone. The field lens, which is considerably larger in diameter and facing the objective, only serves to enlarge the visual field so that the total real intermediate image is visible. You can easily convince yourself of this if you remove the field lens just once: the visual field is now much smaller.

An uncomplicated eyepiece of the Huygenian type consists of only these two (plano-convex) lenses and is therefore rather inexpensive. In

between these two lenses is a perforated circular metal ring—the *visual field diaphragm*. If objective and eyepiece are properly balanced and the mechanical tube length is 160 mm, the intermediate image produced by the objective will be exactly on the plane of this diaphragm. As its name indicates, the visual field diaphragm defines the visual field by eliminating the outermost, unfocused portion of the field of view. If the image is viewed through the eyepiece with a relaxed eye, one should be able to see the image as well as the outermost edge of the diaphragm, providing proper adjustment has been made. The diameter of the visual field diaphragm, expressed in millimeters, is called the *field-of-view number*. For *Huygenian eyepieces*, this field-of-view number is usually

Visual field of an eyepiece. Top: Eyepiece in the normal condition. Bottom: eyepiece without a field lens; the visual field diaphragm has been removed. The specimen is a cross-section of a stem under darkfield illumination

Detail of a marine diatom. The photograph was made of a specimen lying slightly obliquely in the slide. Condenser diaphragm was nearly fully closed, so the object is starting to show the first signs of diffraction. Slight Rheinberg effect.

Left: Huygenian eyepiece.
Right: Compensating eyepiece
from Leica.

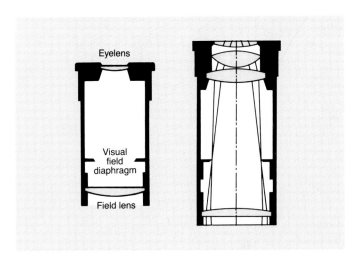

Eyelens

Visual
field
diaphragm

Field lens

around 15. Simple Huygenian eyepieces are used with low- to medium-power achromats. With achromats of higher magnification or other kinds of objectives, the edges of the image will show annoying color distortions. To compensate for such distortion (the source of the name *compensating eyepiece*), you must replace the eyepiece by one in which the eyelens and the field lens consist of compound lens systems. Such eyepieces are, of course, much more expensive.

To eliminate the remaining distortion, manufacturers have finely adjusted the objectives together with the eyepieces. For that reason, it is not wise to buy objective–eyepiece combinations that have not undergone such fine-tuning. If you have found a good, affordable set of objectives, you should buy the eyepieces that have been specially adjusted to them. Write to the manufacturer for specifics.

Specialized eyepieces
In addition to the Huygenian and compensating eyepieces, Olympus and PZO also have made special *photoeyepieces* that project the intermediate image onto the film plane (that's why they are also called *projection lenses*). These eyepieces make it possible to create a more compact photo tube arrangement.

Wide-angle or *wide-field eye-*

pieces are constructed in such a way that a larger portion of the intermediate image can be seen.

High-eyepoint eyepieces, usually recognizable by the size of their eyelenses, increase the distance between the eyelens and your eyes, so that if you wear eyeglasses, you do not need to remove them when using the microscope. Eyepiece inserts are available that have either a ruler (an *ocular micrometer*), cross-hairs, counting grids, cross-wires, or image-field markers; they are added to the plane of the image-field diaphragm, and are used for different types of photography. The eyelens of such eyepieces usually can be adjusted so that the etched lines on these inserts are in focus.

The correct cover glass thickness

When a low-power objective is used and the numerical aper-

ture does not exceed 0.3 or at the most 0.4, the thickness of a cover glass (cover slip), or even working without one, does not influence the quality of the image viewed or photographed. On the other hand, high-power objectives with high numerical apertures are very "cover-glass sensitive." These objectives are designed in such a way that they compensate for *"cover-glass aberration"* if the thickness of the cover glass is exactly 17 mm. Every deviation, even the very smallest—especially increases in thickness—results in a drastic loss of quality. The choice of the proper cover glass is therefore extremely important, and the acceptable deviations are very narrow (0.17 ± 0.005 mm).

A box of cover glasses that says on the lid *"thickness: 0.17 mm"* often holds some surprises. Trusting is good, checking is better! This is easy to do with a screw micrometer calipers equipped with a vernier scale capable of measuring at least $^5/_{1000}$ mm or, better yet, $^1/_{1000}$ mm.

If you want to save time and effort and if you are using a high-power dry system (40× to 60×), buy an assortment of cover glasses. Buying an assortment means that the manufacturer has done the measuring for you, so these are therefore much more expensive. Lastly, a tip that I have learned from experience. The required cover glass thickness of 0.17 mm includes, if we want to be precise, the thickness of the mounting medium and of the specimen, which amounts to about 0.02 mm. This would mean that the optimal thickness of the cover glass should really be between 0.15 mm and

0.16 mm. When you shop for presorted cover glasses, make sure that this thickness is included in the selection. It is much better to clean and take care of expensive cover glasses than to buy cheap ones!

Useful versus "empty" magnification

Let's say you want to magnify an object 400 times. Your objective of 40× and eyepiece of 10× is the choice that comes to mind first. A combination of 20× objective and a 20× eyepiece, or a 16× objective and a 25× eyepiece would, while giving the same magnification, reduce the sharpness of the image. The rule of thumb, therefore, is to choose an objective that has as much re-

solving power as possible, and match it with an eyepiece of lower magnification. All the eyepiece does is magnify the image produced by the objective. It does not add any new information to what's already there. Using high-power eyepieces often produces "optical emptiness" (see, for instance, page 96, bottom right). Strangely enough, one is under the impression when looking at these theoretically "empty" magnifications that there are more details visible than seems to be the case when using the prescribed low-power eyepiece. In other words, don't take the term "useful magnification" too seriously, just make sure that viewing an object with a high-power eyepiece does not become a habit. For example, I routinely work with wide-field eyepieces that produce a 10× magnification, at the most.

Polarization

Polarization filters are used in photography to adjust for

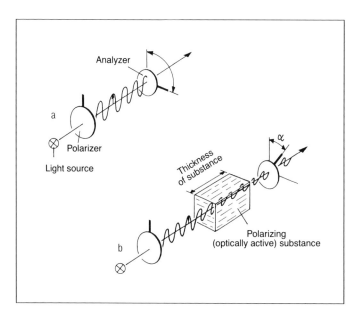

Polarization effect:
a) Perpendicular polarizers block out all light.
b) Polarization with an optically active substance in the ray path shows that a portion of the light comes through.

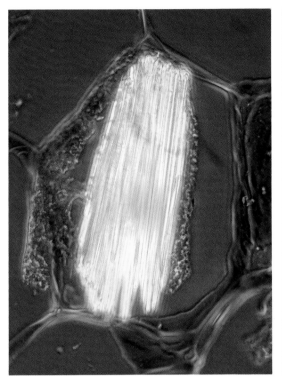

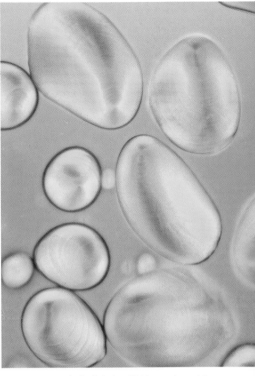

Left: Polarized light reveals oxalate crystals in a plant cell.

Right: Potato starch in polarized light under monochromatic illumination produced with interference filters.

glare, for instance from the water's surface. In microscopy, one polarization filter (the polarizer) is attached below the condenser and a second polarization filter (the analyzer) is placed between the objective and eyepiece; if need be, directly on the eyepiece. If the analyzer is turned in such a way that it is positioned perpendicularly to the polarizer ($\alpha = 90°$; see drawing a on the preceding page); no light will penetrate the analyzer and the result is a *darkfield*. If a specimen that has certain polarization qualities is put in between the polarizer and the analyzer , some light will penetrate and structures will be-

come visible (for instance, those from layered biological structures like striated muscle fibers, connective tissue, tendons, and bone tissues, as well as potato starch (see drawing b on the opposite page). I recommend monochromatic illumination via an interference filter. It is also possible to guide the ray path through a *retardation plate* (or auxiliary object), a small piece of optically anisotropic material (cellophane tape will suffice). A *compensator* is even better; it is a retardation plate whose optical pathlength can be adjusted, made of a birefringent mineral like gypsum, mica, or quartz. Beautiful interference

colors can be produced in this way when a normal white light is used. If both polarizers are turned towards each other at a certain angle, as illustrated in the drawing at left (page 34), very specific effects can be produced as far as depth and intensity of color are concerned (see the photos on page 39).

Phase contrast

Light microscopy distinguishes between amplitude-changing materials and phase-changing materials.

35

Amplitude-changing materials. Amplitude-changing materials reduce or block incoming light rays. As a light wave moves through these objects, the amplitude (A_1, the maximum extent of a light wave vibration) is reduced (see part "a" of the figure below). The amplitude of the light passing through the object is less than that of light that passes by the object. We see the object because it appears darker or colored (only particular wavelengths are allowed to pass through the object) against the background. Our eyes and photographic film are very capable of detecting small amplitude differences by the changes in brightness. Typical amplitude-changing materials are thick-cut and dyed specimens.

Phase-changing materials— for example, thin, undyed sections, fragile microorganisms

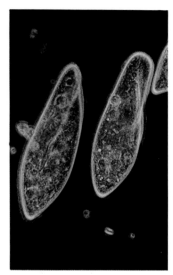

Example of a phase-contrast photo of a single-celled animal, *Paramecium caudatum*.

Amplitudes and phases of light waves that pass through and outside materials (see text).

and the like—hardly reduce the amplitude of light and therefore do not sufficiently contrast with the surrounding space. However, a phase shift does occur in the light waves that pass through the material, compared to the waves that pass outside the material (phase difference, ϕ); see part b in the drawing below.

Unfortunately, neither the human retina nor photographic film is able to detect phase differences. Contrasts are created only if there is a method that changes phase differences into amplitude differences—that is, differences in brightness. And, indeed, several methods exist that convert phase differences into amplitude differences. A detailed, theoretical explanation is not possible in the context of this book.

The phase shift necessary to

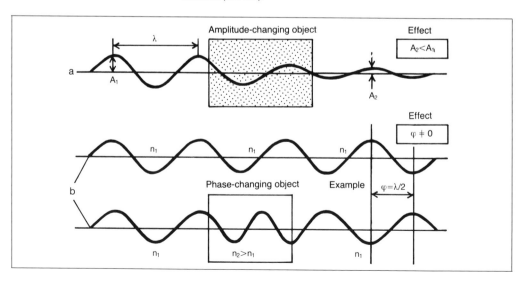

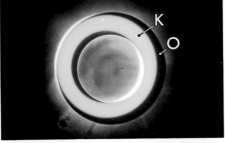

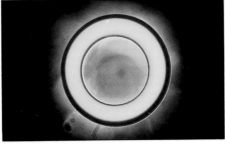

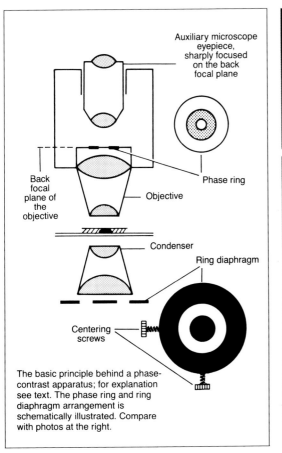

Auxiliary microscope eyepiece, sharply focused on the back focal plane

Phase ring

Back focal plane of the objective

Objective

Condenser

Ring diaphragm

Centering screws

The basic principle behind a phase-contrast apparatus; for explanation see text. The phase ring and ring diaphragm arrangement is schematically illustrated. Compare with photos at the right.

generate phase contrast differences is, in practical terms, accomplished by a *phase ring*: a very thin, ring-shaped layer of metal applied to the objective at its back focal plane. The light beam that illuminates the object must also be ring-shaped and is slightly smaller than the phase ring. This is done with a ring-shaped annulus placed in the condenser. The ring-shaped beam of light from the condenser annulus must be centered within the phase ring to obtain the best contrast. Centering of the two rings is accomplished by shifting the condenser ring annulus with the aid of special centering screws in the condenser. With the aid of a special eyepiece called a *centering telescope*, this adjustment can be easily carried out (see photos above). If the images of both rings are on top of each other, the phase contrast is properly adjusted (bottom photo).

Pictures of a condenser-ring diaphragm (K) and a phase ring (O) at the back focal plane of the objective, photographed with the help of a centering telescope, a special eyepiece. Above: not adjusted; middle: badly adjusted; below: precise, concentrically adjusted. Such an adjusting procedure should be repeated every time an objective or condenser is changed, because improperly adjusted equipment results in poor images.

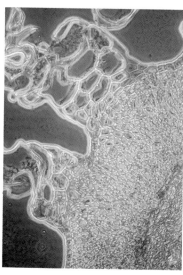

Examples of phase-contrast photos of cross-sections of botanical specimens. Left: soft tissue of a water lily showing inner "hairs." Right: cross-section of a hair from a pumpkin stem.

Below left: cross-section of an inflorescence of a tulip.
Below right: cross-section of star-shaped tissue of a rush.

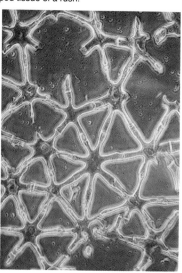

Interference contrast

Interference contrast is achieved by sending one light ray through an object and a second past the object, exactly as illustrated in the drawing on the right-hand page. Then, both light rays are "combined" in an interference pattern, which in turn creates the contrast. The (routine) procedure is as follows (numbers refer to the diagram at the right): With the aid of a Wollaston prism (7/8), one light ray is split in two adjoining rays (A) and (B), which are then sent through the condenser (6), slide (5), and objective (4); because the distance between the two rays is below the limit of resolution only one image is seen. The double ray is then again changed into one ray with the aid of a second Wollaston prism (2/3). Since a polarizer (9) and analyzer (1) are used in this optical system, polarization effects also are created.

By shifting the second prism (2/3) relative to the first prism (7/8), polarization colors can be created and also different background colors: from white to yellow and from red to blue. Organs within the specimen will then appear in contrasting colors, depending on their thickness, density, and refractive index. This gives you a wonderful opportunity to let your imagination fly. You can also scan a preparation in contrast-rich "optical sections."

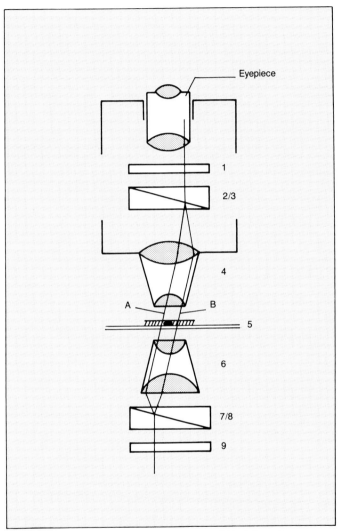

Eyepiece

1

2/3

4

A   B

5

6

7/8

9

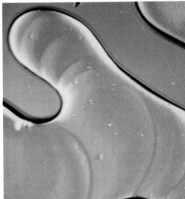

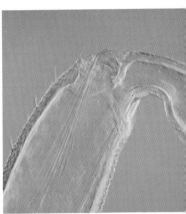

Above: Main features of interference contrast. The individual elements are numbered and discussed in the text. The paths of the rays are illustrated schematically; in reality the distance between both partial rays, A and B, is only part of $\frac{1}{1000}$ mm.

Right: example of interference-contrast photos.
Top: mounting medium hardened in layers.
Middle: joint of the leg of a mite, with delicate muscle tissue.
Bottom: cross-section of a piece of wood with color transitions. The dots are particularly well contrasted (green against red).

Fluorescence contrast

When exposed to a high-power, short-wave ultraviolet or blue light ("exciter light"), certain molecules will emit longer-wavelength light (fluorescent light), and, for instance, appear a light-yellow color. This phenomenon of objects, in which they become fluorescent under certain circumstances, also has been used in microscopic research. For instance, we know that chlorophyll has a red fluorescence. When we illuminate a botanical specimen using an excitation filter (which filters out every light except specific short-wave blue light), and photograph it with the aid of a barrier filter (which almost exclusively allows only fluorescent light to come through), the chlorophyll-containing organelles appear brilliant red.

Nonfluorescent tissues can be made fluorescent with the selective use of fluorescent stains. Many structures may be discovered using such a procedure. For instance, parts of the so-called cell skeleton that are invisible under normal circumstances can be made visible by using immunofluorescence. The black-and-white photo on the top of page 41 even shows the delicate filaments surrounding the nucleus.

Transmitted-light fluorescence microscopes (drawing a, below) are today replaced by epi-fluorescence microscopes (drawing b). In the latter case, the objective of the microscope acts as the condenser for the exciter light and as an objective for the fluorescent light.

Principal paths of light in fluorescence apparatus: (a) transmitted light fluorescence; (b) incident light fluorescence (see text).

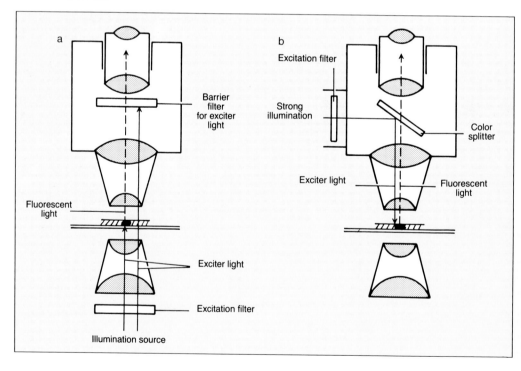

Fluorescence equipment requires high-power illumination and is very expensive. To achieve the same effect one can, however, make do by improvising with less expensive methods. Use transmitted light and, as an excitation filter between the condenser and the illuminator, use a very strong blue filter (the best is deep-blue cobalt glass). Just put a strong orange filter as a barrier filter on the eyelens of the eyepiece. Turn up the illumination to its highest level, use a low-power objective, and turn out all light in the room. The above-mentioned red fluorescence seen in chloroplasts demonstrates the point very well and can even be photographed, with exposure times from a few seconds to one minute.

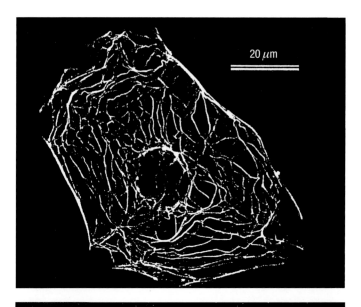

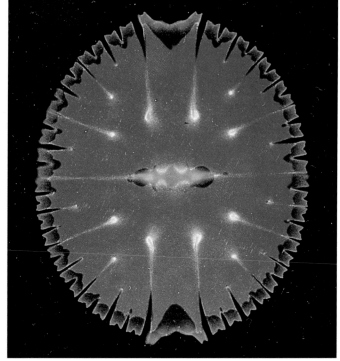

Above: a high-contrast photocopy (see page 69) of a black-and-white photo. Delicate—and usually invisible—filaments of a cell's 'skeleton" become visible with the use of fluorescence contrast.

Below: Desmid *Micrasterias*. Fluorescence contrast. A chloroplast, green under normal illumination, turns conspicuously red when fluorescence contrast is used.

ILLUMINATION

Light sources

The microscopist differentiates between *transmitted* and *reflected illumination*. *Reflected* illumination is used for objects that are impenetrable to light, like rocks and exoskeletons of insects. *Transmitted* illumination can be adjusted for darkfield or brightfield microscopy. First let us discuss the most important methods for simple transmitted illumination.

Daylight

Turn the flat side of the mirror (not the concave side) to a bright spot in the sky, not to the sun, but rather to a bright cloud. (Deep-blue sky is not as good.) The result is a beautiful, even illumination. When using a very low-power objective, you might do away with the condenser altogether. Set the condenser as high as possible, lowering it if necessary afterward—for instance, if structures like the edge of the cloud appear in the visual field.

Plug-in Illuminator

Instead of the mirror, an illuminator with a light bulb mounted in a housing with frosted glass, with a place where a blue glass disk can be added in front of the light (to adjust the long-wave reddish light of the bulb to daylight), can be used.

Sea worm with multiple bristles. Rheinberg illumination was adjusted until the delicate spines became shiny and were clearly visible.

Plug-in illumination from Hertel & Reuss.

The light from the source (or through the frosted glass) is transmitted to the object plane. As in the above-mentioned daylight circumstances, one may speak of "critical illumination." For that, the condenser must be as high as possible. The relatively high temperatures that are created can be somewhat reduced by adding a heat-shield filter into the filter holder of the condenser.

This type of illumination can be very gentle and comfortable and, as far as light intensity is concerned, is sufficient for medium magnification.

Low-Voltage Illumination with Auxiliary Mirrors

Correct Köhler illumination (see page 46) can be tricky and time-consuming. For that reason, some manufacturers have decided to include either plug-in or built-in low-voltage illuminators that are permanently focused, in which the light rays are guided by concave mirrors for their student and teaching microscopes.

Low-Voltage Illumination with Auxiliary Lenses

Low-voltage lights, either separately housed in a fixture or permanently built into the base of the microscope, which is more practical, produce a very bright light, using low power (for instance, 6 volts

Low-voltage light mounted on a separate base from Zeiss. F: vertically adjustable filter holder. K: auxiliary lens. This is an example of a classical illuminator.

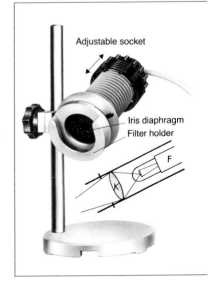

Adjustable socket

Iris diaphragm
Filter holder

F

K

and 5 amps = 30 watts). Such a light produces particularly good images, with sharp contrast.

More-high-powered light sources (for instance, high-powered halogen lights with 12 volts and 8 amps, thus about 100 watts) and auxiliary lenses are housed in a special housing because of the heat that is created during operation. Instead of such an arrangement one can use a less powerful light source with a lens mount, which can, if necessary, be inserted into the base of the microscope. It is very important, when using such a device, that

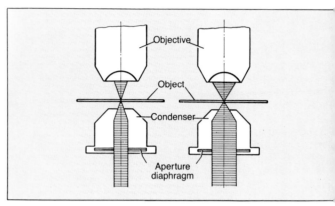

Effects of the condenser diaphragm (see text for details).

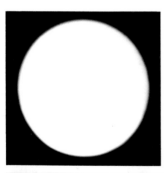

Top: View of the objective's back lens; eyepiece removed. Bottom: View of the back lens when the condenser diaphragm is closed down to two-thirds of the diameter shown above.

you are able to center the auxiliary lens facing the microscope or the bulb, so the mount should have two adjusting screws.

Condenser

A condenser is a system of lenses of extremely short focal length and a very high luminous intensity. The condenser collects the light and illuminates the object from below. However, its main purpose is not so much to increase the illumination of the image (which could be more easily accomplished with a more powerful light); rather, the condenser makes it possible to take full advantage of a high numerical aperture of the objective. The light beam is focused on the object plane and then diverges again. If the angle of the beam is wide (condenser diaphragm is open wide), it will also meet the objective at a wide angle: large aperture. When the condenser diaphragm is opened less, the angle is reduced and the effec-

tive aperture becomes smaller, in spite of the nominal aperture engraved in the objective. At the same time, the illumination of the specimen is reduced and depth of field is increased. The contrast of the image is also increased. Ideally, the aperture of the objective and the condenser should—in theory—correspond with each other. If the condenser aperture is considerably larger than the objective aperture, the quality of the image is much reduced because of excess radiation and the image becomes weaker. If, on the other hand, the condenser aperture is distinctly smaller than that of the objective—which, after all, needs a light beam with a particular aperture angle β (see page 28)—the beam reaching the objective is too narrow. In that case, the resolving power for which the objective is designed cannot be achieved: the effort expended in designing a high-powered objective is wasted if the wrong illumination is chosen! One ought never lose sight of this correlation. In practical terms, and in order to avoid glare, condensers with large numerical aperture require more stopping down than that which, in theory, is recommended. For that reason, and in most cases, a simple two-lens condenser with an aperture that might either be somewhat smaller than the objective aperture, or whose aperture can be closed down to ⅔ of that of the objective aperture, is perfectly good. A condenser aperture of 0.95 (for an immersion objective) or even only 0.6 (for a dry system) is sufficient.

To properly adjust the condenser aperture: open the aperture diaphragm, remove the eyepiece and look at the well-illuminated back lens of the objective. Now, slowly close the aperture diaphragm until it becomes visible. Now the condenser aperture and the objective aperture are identical. The next step is to close the diaphragm until the diameter is ⅔ of what was visible of the original illuminated back lens. If you close the diaphragm further than that (which is very tempting, because contrast and depth of field seem to increase), you are reducing the resolving power. Closing of the diaphragm, therefore, has unintended effects (diminished brightness and decreased resolution) as well as intended effects (increased depth of focus, increased contrast). Closing the diaphragm a little to halfway is good. If the diaphragm is closed too much, undue emphasis is placed on contrast, and in addition, primary diffraction patterns, which create double or multiple margins of the image, appear, which in turn produce images of nonexistent structures, so to say (compare the photos on page 32 and page 79).

Therefore, only decrease the opening of the condenser diaphragm and lower the condenser when sharp contrast is a must, as in the case of viewing delicate protozoa—for example, amoebae and

Closing the iris diaphragm decreases the brightness of the image. However, *under no circumstances* should you use the diaphragm to adjust brightness! If you have too much brightness, decrease the intensity of the illuminator. Usually reddish overtones appear due to spectral shifts; only modern phase procedures will eliminate such effects. If this is annoying, brightness can be lessened by adding neutral-density filters.

When an extremely low-powered objective is used, remove the front lens (the smaller top lens) of the condenser; otherwise the margins of the field of view will not be illuminated. Extremely weak magnifications ($1\times$ to approximately $5\times$) are either produced without the use of a condenser or, better yet, with special spectacle-glass (simple lens) condensers. In that case the aperture diaphragm loses its effect. Condensers can be attached or removed by sliding them out of their housing; always rotate them slightly when

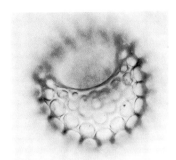

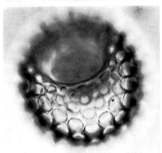

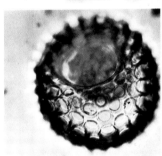

Influence of the condenser diaphragm. Above: diaphragm has been opened too far (excess radiation); Middle: diaphragm closed to ⅔; Below: diaphragm closed as far as possible creates strong contrasts and depth of field, but lessens resolution power. Subject: piece of a radiolarian.

removing them. Adjustments on more expensive equipment are done with the help of a gear mechanism. For everyday use that is more practical and faster. In addition, you should be able to center the condenser. For this, its housing should have two adjustment screws. That is very important with Köhler illumination.

Principles of Köhler illumination

This system gives the microscopist ideal illumination. It was developed by August Köhler (1866–1948). It consists of two interdependent steps in which images are created (paths of rays):

1. Forming an image of the filament of a low-voltage light bulb on the diaphragm plane of the condenser (aperture diaphragm) by means of collector lenses.

2. Adjusting the position of the condenser so that the field diaphragm is visible in the object plane.

Step 1 results in an optimal light path and the best possible use of the light source. Step 2 reduces the illuminated field to its most suitable diameter and thereby prevents bothersome reflections that would otherwise appear. With the Köhler

illumination system we must therefore examine two diaphragms. The *condenser diaphragm* (also called the iris or aperture diaphragm) adjusts the diameter of the light beam to the aperture diameter of the objective. The *illuminated field diaphragm* serves to reduce the illuminated field and reduces glare (excess radiation).

The Köhler Procedure

This, in technical jargon, signifies proper adjustment of the Köhler illumination. This multistep method should be practiced until it becomes second nature.

1. Centering the Light Bulb. The first step is to center the bulb in its housing, if this has not already been done by the manufacturer. If you have a separate microscope light, project the filament onto a wall and turn the bulb around its own axis. Using the two adjustment screws, align the filament with the optical axis. If that has been accomplished, the projected image will remain centered without creating a halo.

If the microscope has a built-in light source, put a piece of typewriter paper on top of the illuminator opening and center the light source with the adjustment screws. If the lamp housing has a mirror, the image and the mirror image of the bulb's filament should dovetail.

2. Imaging of the Filament. Focus on a flat-field specimen, perhaps a microscopic cross-section. Close the aperture diaphragm as much

A sharp image of the filament is projected on a piece of paper that has been put on the diaphragm plane of the condenser (aperture diaphragm).

as possible, while keeping the iris of the illuminated field diaphragm totally open. Now, adjust the path of rays by moving the collector lens at the lamp's housing (or by adjusting the mirror, if you are using an unattached illuminator) until you have a sharp image of the filament on the closed aperture diaphragm (or on a round piece of paper placed on the aperture diaphragm). Such an image should not extend beyond the margin of the dia-

Lamp adjustment. Left: insufficient adjustment. Right: optimal dovetail of the image and the mirror image.

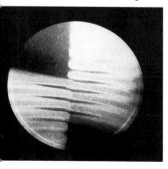
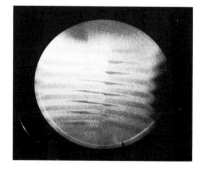

phragm, nor should it be smaller than about ⅔ of the diameter of the diaphragm.

3. Centering the Condenser. Open the aperture diaphragm of the condenser as far as possible and close the illuminated field diaphragm until it appears somewhere in the field in the form of a faded lighted circle.

Using small up-and-down movements, adjust the position of the condenser, using its rack-and-pinion knob, until the edges of the illuminated field diaphragm are in sharp focus. The next step is to adjust the condenser, with the help of both adjustment screws, until the illuminated field diaphragm is accurately centered. (If you have little experience, this procedure is easier when you use a larger diaphragm diameter—one that will produce contour margins closer to the image field— rather than a smaller one).

If the edges on one side of the field diaphragm are red and they are blue on the other side, there is a disturbing eccentricity somewhere in the light path. Repeat the procedure as outlined above, if need be several times, to improve on the result.

4. Adjusting the Illuminated Field Diaphragm. Now open the illuminated field diaphragm until the edges have just about disappeared from the field of vision. That is all there is to this step in the adjustment. By adjustment of the field diaphragm, parts of the specimen outside the field of

view are not illuminated. This eliminates glare caused by light scattered by objects outside the field of view and, to an astounding degree, improves the contrast. This is one of the two "basic tricks" of Köhler illumination.

5. Adjusting the Aperture Diaphragm. Last, close the aperture diaphragm of the condenser somewhat, until about ⅔ of the diameter of the back lens of the objective is still visible. This is easily done (see the photos on page 44) with the eyepiece removed. These are the necessary steps for adjusting Köhler illumination.

By small movements of the condenser up and down and also opening and closing the iris of the condenser diaphragm (always observing the above-mentioned limits) microscopists can vary the contrast of an image very specifically to their own needs. The entire Köhler procedure must be repeated after each objective change (turn of the rotatable nosepiece) whenever optimal illumination is required. This is particularly important when making adjustments for phase contrast.

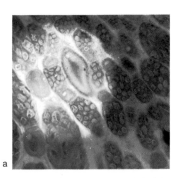

a

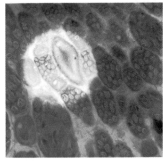

b

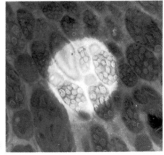

c

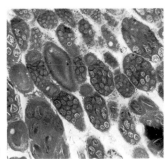

d

Centering and focusing the condenser. From top to bottom: (a) Illuminated field diaphragm eccentric and insufficiently focused. (b) Illuminated field diaphragm eccentric and sharply focused. (c) Illuminated field diaphragm centered. (d) After opening the illuminated field diaphragm, the specimen is evenly and completely illuminated.

Of course, Step 1, when done carefully, does not have to be repeated for a while.

Proper Height Adjustment of the Condenser

Because the condenser is so easily adjusted and the images change so drastically when that is done, the less experienced microscopist might think that this is the way to adjust the intensity of light and the contrast.

However, as has already been mentioned, one ought to make use of this possibility only with care and sparingly, and leave the condenser generally in or near the position that is required for Köhler illumination. When in doubt, it is

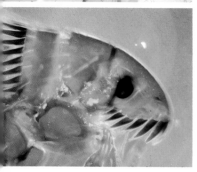

The head of a dog flea (*Ctenocephalides canis*). Top: in normal brightfield illumination. Bottom: photographed in mixed light with oblique illumination.

best to keep the condenser *as high as possible*. The condenser should only be lowered when glare or any other distortion in the visual field has appeared while it is close to or near its highest position.

Types of illumination

Transmitted Light— Brightfield Illumination

This is the type of illumination we have been discussing so far and the one that is best accomplished by using the Köhler illumination method.

Oblique Illumination

An Abbe substage (found in better, alas older, microscopes) can produce oblique illumination in the following way: a gear mechanism "decentralizes" the iris of the condenser, meaning that it is moved out of the optical axis of the microscope.

However, the same effect can also be achieved by the following extremely simple means: take a black strip of paper and cut or punch out holes from it ranging from about 0.5 to 1.5 cm (.2 in. to .6 in.). If you position this strip on the filter holder below the condenser, it is easy to put this "hole diaphragm" in any position you like. First, start to locate a smaller and then a greater eccentricity that points

in one particular direction— for instance, to the right, the left or at an angle—and then move the diaphragm opening in a circle around the center of the optical axis, all the while observing the changes of the "pseudosteroscopic" effect.

The specimen is now in a bright field but obliquely illuminated, which might possibly make structures visible that could not be seen with directly transmitted light. However, the overall contrast of the image is somewhat reduced. The images can be very beautiful and often produce photographs with extra flair (see photo page 53).

Relief Illumination

If you move this "hole diaphragm" away from the optical axis even further, you will quickly reach a point where the object begins to seem to lift itself off the background, because one edge has darkened, while the opposite is lighter. It looks as if the object is casting a shadow. This "pseudo-three-dimensional" impression of an image can really be a surprise. As illustrated on page 55, this process can be carried to an extreme with a 3-D condenser.

Transmitted Light and Darkfield Illumination

Here the condenser diaphragm and illuminated field diaphragm are opened all the way. Next, add a clear glass disk, or Plexiglas disk, to which a smaller dark paper disk has been glued centrally, to the filter holder of the con-

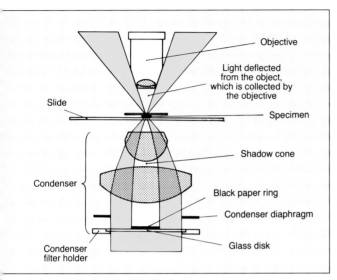

Ray path in transmitted-light darkfield illumination.

House scorpion *Chelifer cancroides* in (top) brightfield illumination with yellow filter and (bottom) in darkfield illumination.

denser. (A perfect circle is easy to make with a divider and a pair of curved nail scissors for cutting.) Have three or four different sizes of these paper disks on hand, starting with a central, black circle about half the size of the glass disk, and making some that are even smaller. One of these will surely fit your purpose. Raise or lower the condenser until the specimen appears shiny and bright on a totally dark background. Specimens like diatoms, radiolarians, and also ciliates can be particularly well observed and photographed in this way.

The drawing above illustrates the path of rays. The numerical aperture of the condenser must be higher than that of the objective; the condenser diaphragm is open all the way. The remaining marginal rays will give bright illumination to the object, but they will not reach the objective directly. The central rays are blocked out and that's why the background appears so dark. This not only looks very beautiful, but under special circumstances might also reveal more information than would be available otherwise. For instance, delicate structures like blue-green algae and diatoms are only visible with darkfield illumination. As simple as this technique is, some experimenting is necessary.

Today there are commercial darkfield condensers available, some with lower and some with higher numerical apertures. The former might well

49

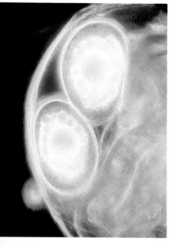

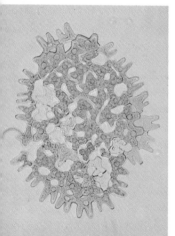

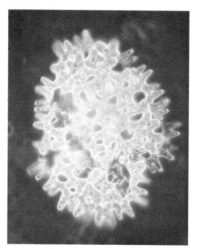

Examples of different kinds of lighting. Upper left: Two embryos inside the brood chamber of waterflea *Alona costata* under darkfield illumination. Upper right: Water flea *(Daphnia longispina)* under darkfield illumination.

Lower left: normal brightfield photograph. Lower right: mixed illumination with darkfield character. Both photographs of an aberrant form of *Pediastrum duplex*.

be ignored, since objective magnification up to $20 \times$ dark-field illumination is easily produced by improvising with paper disks. For more powerful magnification, like $40 \times$ or $60 \times$, you will need a fairly expensive darkfield condenser with a high numerical aperture. The ray path moves be-

tween a smaller spherical surface (mirrored on the outside) and a larger spherical surface (mirrored on the inside; see the diagram on page 56). Such a mirror condenser is only useful for certain numerical aperture objectives, and can't be used for general purposes.

Special color effects

Optical Coloring of Objects

If you choose a tinted glass disk instead of a clear one for darkfield illumination—for example, a yellow filter to which a dark paper disk has been glued—the object will have the color of the filter (here, yellow) and appear on a dark background (see the photo on the bottom of page 52).

Colored Background with Darkfield Illumination

It is possible to proceed in the reverse way: exchange the black paper disk, for instance, for a strong blue filter (several layers of paper filter glued together; avoid streaking the glue), and the object will appear bright on a dark-blue background (see the photo on page 53).

Rheinberg Illumination

As just outlined above, the simple but effective darkfield illumination with a central stop made of black paper will show a light object on a dark background if a colored filter is inserted in the diaphragm holder; objects are displayed brightly illuminated with a colored background if a colored filter is used instead of the black disk stop. Both types of illumination can be combined: you can use deep-red film to make a central filter disk (if need be, gluing together as many layers of film as are needed to create the required depth of color, always avoiding creating streaks of glue), adding a perfectly fitting blue diaphragm ring. If the iris diaphragm is opened all the way, the specimen will have light-blue margins against a red background (see photo on page 52, top left). Experiment with as many contrasting colors as you like. Such double

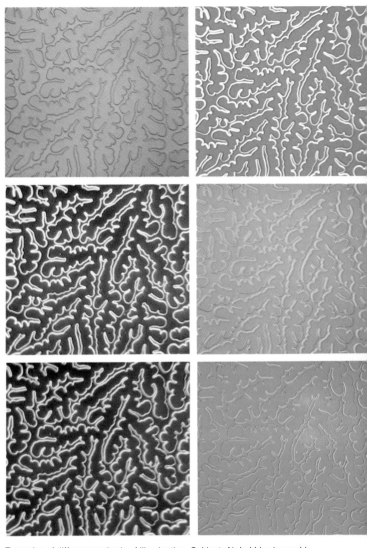

Examples of different methods of illumination. Subject: Air bubbles in an old slide. Top left: brightfield, with the diaphragm very closed down. Middle left: darkfield illumination. Lower left: Rheinberg illumination, yellow/red against black central stop. Top right: Rheinberg illumination, white against a deep blue central stop. Middle right: Rheinberg illumination; red against delicate blue central stop. Lower right: Rheinberg illumination, white against deep-red central stop (see text and photos on page 52).

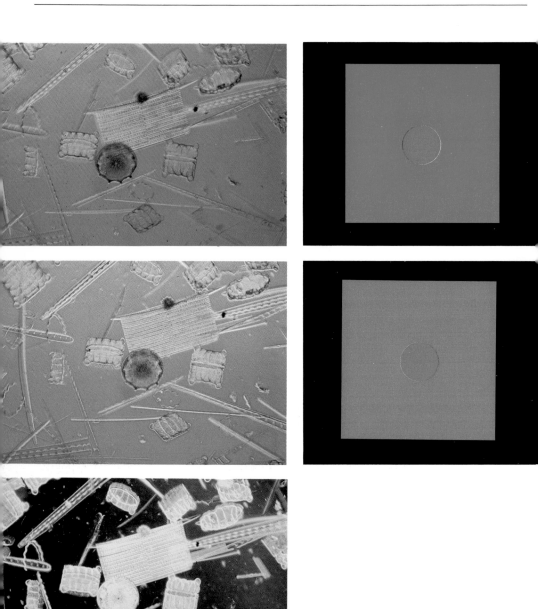

Examples of Rheinberg illumination. Top left: diatoms, light-blue against red background. Top right: the filter used in the top left sample. Middle left: diatoms, light red against light-blue background. Middle right: the filter used in middle left sample. Bottom: shows the same subject photographed in transmitted light, with a yellow filter and a black central stop (darkfield effect).

filters are easy to make if the contrasting films are put between two thin pieces of glass and framed. Of course, this slide is unwieldy when you try to put it into the filter housing of the condenser. Adding a special filter ring (see top photo, page 14) about 5 mm below the condenser will solve this problem. However, always make sure that there is sufficient depth of color in the central stop, otherwise you will not achieve the desired dark-field effect.

By changing the diameter of the central stop, you can also, as in our example, produce a "red-colored" object that appears on a blue background, or one with dark-blue margins and a deep-red background. Also, changing the distance between the aperture diaphragm and the filter can change the appearance of an object. Lowering or raising the condenser also creates different effects, and small changes in the aperture setting can reduce the brightness of the colored margins. If the height of the condenser is changed, colors and darkfield effects may change rapidly. Lastly, placing a filter slightly off-center will produce lateral 3-dimensional illumination.

By careful "optical staining" a diatom and viewing it in slightly oblique illumination one can, for instance, produce delicate spatial structures with great clarity and 3-dimensional effects, colored differently than the surrounding field (see the photo on the bottom of page 32).

You can even go further; for instance, make a ring diaphragm that has 2 or 4 sections in blue and green, positioned opposite each other. As a result, your specimen takes on a red appearance with partially blue and partially green edges.

You may arrange two concentric ring diaphragms of different colors around the central black stop (experiment by choosing one that is a little bit "too small"). Ideally, the specimen will appear in the color of the inner filter against a dark background, surrounded by edges in the color of the outer filter.

While playing with all these color combinations, all kinds of extreme effects and color distortions are possible. Nowhere in microscopy are we able to experiment as much. Nowhere, however (let's be honest), is the danger of creating kitsch as great as here. But, as we all know, kitsch is in the eyes of the beholder. And besides, by no means are we always pursuing scientific goals, particularly when microscopy is a hobby.

Mixed-light illumination

It is very easy to combine brightfield and darkfield illumination by putting a central stop (a large, round black paper disk glued to a round glass disk) in the filter holder and moving it more or less eccentrically. The result is that a larger or smaller portion of the visual field will appear bright

and the rest dark, depending on the setting of the stop.

Specimens that lie in the middle also will appear partially bright and partially dark and often take on a 3-dimensional appearance. If a specimen has delicate appendages, bristles, or protoplasmic rays, it is possible to arrange the bright–dark boundaries in such a way that the rays are primarily in the dark field and the "body" in the bright field.

When using mirror illumination, the illumination of such boundaries can easily be accomplished with a concave

Radiolarian, white light against blue background; oblique illumination.

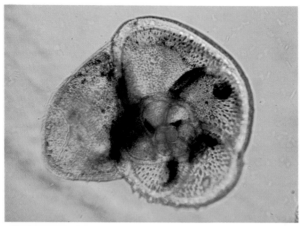

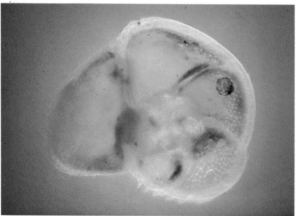

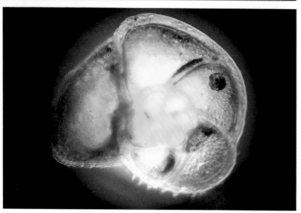

mirror that is shifted laterally. Last, one can close the illuminated field diaphragm and lower the condenser until the border of the diaphragm appears in the visual field as a bright-dark boundary. A diffuse border with delicate, colored margins is created by lowering the condenser even further (see the photos on the left).

The visual effect of a specimen viewed through a microscope depends to a great degree on the illumination employed.

It is possible to produce two different effects. On one hand, each method of illumination can emphasize certain details; on the other hand, when playing with different types of illumination, we are able to produce varying and very impressive graphic effects. For instance, the photo on the bottom of page 54 is the result, strictly speaking, of an "illumination mistake," but it still has a beauty all its own.

Foraminifera of the genus *Globigerina* in different illuminations: Top: brightfield, with small diaphragm opening. Middle: darkfield against light-blue background. Bottom: darkfield illumination with an almost closed illuminated field diaphragm and the condenser lowered).

3-D illumination

The stepped-mirror condenser from Hund is a very interesting instrument. It is named for the (somewhat exaggerated) 3-dimensional effect it creates. Here, the large spherical surface, mirrored on the inside, is shaped in steplike fashion (see the drawing on the bottom of page 56). Depending on the path of the ray, the numerical aperture may be set between 0.3 and 0.9, which allows for universal adaptation with every common dry system. This is accomplished by using different height adjustments and gradual changes in position in brightfield as well as darkfield illumination and with any number of transitional or mixed illuminations. This is an ideal instrument for a microscopist who gets easily bored with the conventional methods of illumination and likes to experiment and play around.

Since, when compared to the normal darkfield condenser, illustrated in the drawing on the top left, only the reflection from a small metal ball is used in the 3-D con-

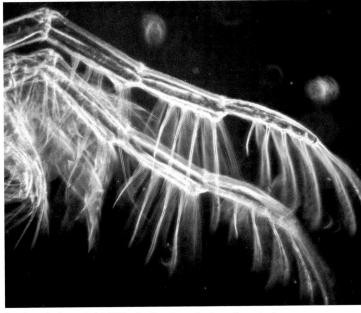

An effect similar to darkfield illumination shows the legs of a water flea, *Leptodora kindtii*; the bristlelike covering is particularly well shown. Compare with photo on p. 142.

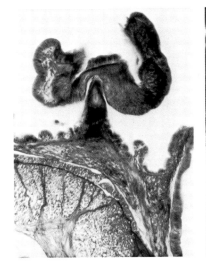
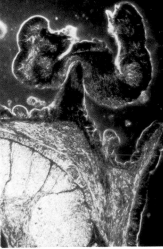

The sucker of a cuttlefish. Left: with normal condenser. Right: with a 3-D condenser.

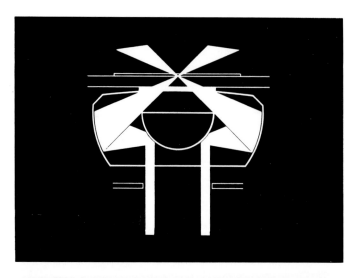

Path of light rays in a darkfield condenser from Zeiss, where the reflection of light is produced by two different mirrored planes (see page 49 and 50 also).

denser, these condensers have very weak illumination.

The last method of microscope illumination to be discussed is incident illumination. In the case of low magnification, the effect on the image produced is not much different from that of the darkfield illumination (see the photo on page 52). For that reason, incident illumination is only used in very special circumstances.

Incident illumination

Incident illumination is needed when dealing with opaque objects: minerals, rocks, metal surfaces, chitin covers, snail shells, and the like. As with every other special procedure, here, too, we can use highly technical (and very expensive) equipment, such as special objectives through which light is directed around the lens with a ring-shaped illumination system (for example, the Ultropak system from Leitz). You can also reflect the light directly

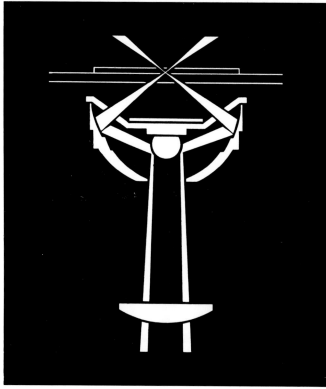

Path of light rays in a stepped-mirror condenser from Hund. The large mirrored inner surface is constructed in steplike fashion, which allows the light rays to be reflected from different sectors toward the specimen, depending on the height adjustment.

The combination of incident and transmitted illumination creates a particularly impressive image. The "wing" of a maple seed was photographed under low magnification (Olympus 1 × objective) with a combination of blue transmitted light (tissue) and red, grazing incident light (veins).

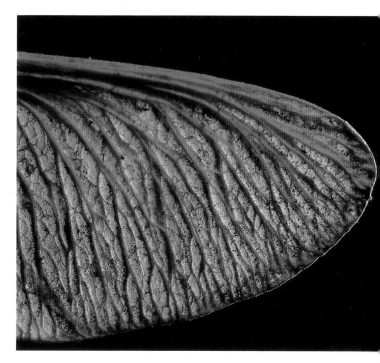

via a partially silvered mirror either below or above the objective.

Under low-power magnification, which also means with that the distance between the front lens of the objective and the specimen is not too short, incident illumination is not difficult to adjust. Instead of lighting from below, illuminate obliquely from above. This is easily done with a conventional low-voltage lamp. However, you can also put a spherical Nitraphot lamp 1 meter (39 in.) away and, with the aid of one or two small shaving mirrors, direct the rays onto the specimen.

In some circumstances, consider a combination of incident lighting and colored transmitted illumination. With this method a specimen will stand out against a colored background without the trace of a shadow, as shown in the photos of the *Pilobolus* fungus and the maple seed on this page.

Fungus *(Pilobolus)* showing spore capsule carrier with a black spore capsule; photographed with a combination of incident and transmitted illumination.

Path of light rays in the Ultropak incident illumination objective from Leitz (now Leica).

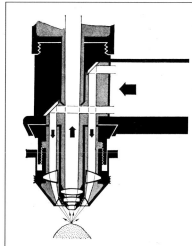

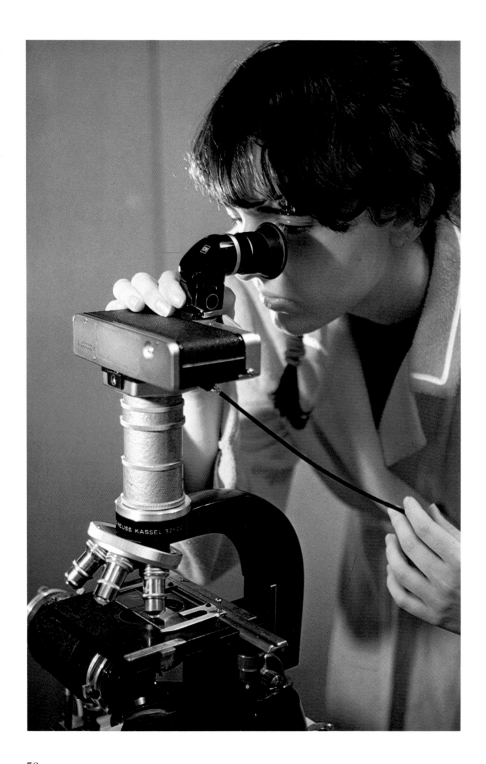

PHOTOMICROGRAPHY

Basic techniques

Large-format cameras

If you want to make oversized photos of still structures (for instance, from histological sections, powdered specimens, or the like) and later turn them into poster-size enlargements, you need to use 8 × 10 inch or 4 × 5 inch color negative sheet film. The necessary equipment is hardly different from the optical systems that have been used for scientific work for over 100 years. However, here we are entering the professional domain of scientific photography.

Hobby photomicrography today uses 35-mm reflex cameras almost exclusively.

35-mm Reflex Camera

When a 35-mm reflex camera is mounted at the normal viewing distance of 25 cm (10 in.) above the microscope, a very long intermediate tube is needed. The whole system becomes rather unstable and, because of the small size of the film, you are able to photograph only a small portion of the microscopic image. If the distance is shortened, the microscope is more stable and the portion on the photograph is much larger. However, in order to adjust the focus on the ground glass screen, you must either move the eyepiece further out or raise the tube a bit

Simple photomicrography setup with pre–World War II classic microscope.

more, which causes all the previous optical adjustments of the microscope to be disturbed.

To compensate for this disadvantage, use the following well-tested method (see photo to the right): instead of the normal eyepiece, use a special photo eyepiece or projection eyepiece, like those made by Olympus or PZO, for example, and those made in the past by Leitz and Zeiss. They are usually calibrated to a short projection distance of 12.5 cm (about 5 in.), half of the normal visual distance of 25 cm (10 in.), and thereby guarantee a more stable way of mounting a camera. This system is highly recommended for the hobby microscopist.

Photography without an eyepiece

Good, contrast-rich pictures can be made when the eyepiece is removed altogether. By changing the distance between the specimen and the objective, the intermediate image is produced further up, on a ground glass or the film plane, rather than, as was formerly the case, in the tube. Specially designed eyepieces compensate for the remaining distortions of the objective; however, if less powerful objectives are used and the eyepiece has been removed, and only the central portion of the intermediate image is photographed, it is practically impossible to detect any reduction in the quality of the picture. A great advantage is that small pieces of dust and

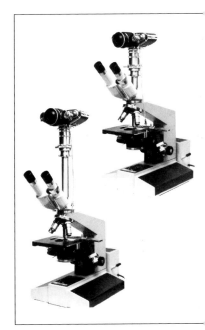

Exacta camera with a focusing eyepiece on a Biolar base from PZO. Left: with long extension and normal eyepiece; Right: short extension with photo eyepiece.

streaks present on the eyepiece are eliminated; otherwise they almost always appear as small spots on the picture. And another advantage: when working with bright parallel light (maybe by using an old slide projector) without the condenser, even the most delicate, often easily overexposed, structures will produce strong, distinct shadows. This process has been found to work extremely well for photos of delicate plankton (as seen on page 69, top photo).

Extension tubes for the 35-mm reflex camera

Listing all the different types available would fill whole books. I will keep the list short by suggesting a certain system that I believe is the best. But I want you to be aware that there are plenty of others that are very solid and often also very affordable. The system I am about to present to you consists of clamp-on attachments and intermediate adapters (1–4 below) like, for instance, the ones offered by Göke. Here are the parts belonging to this system:

1. Rotatable clamp-on attachment (T) for a standard tube diameter of 25 mm with a dovetail ring clamp, which is clamped to the microscope tube and remains

on the microscope. The photo eyepiece is mounted above it.

2. Dovetail ring intermediary piece (R) with an M-42 thread. This fits into (1) and, together with the whole system, is easily removed and adjusted.

3. Set of four M-42 extension rings (Z). The camera, attached to the very top ring, also has M-42 threads (for example, a Praktica camera or something similar) or:

4. Extension tube that connects with M-42 threads to the bayonet mount of the camera (A).

5. A 35-mm reflex camera back with bayonet mount.

6. Slide-in angular viewfinder, if the camera does not have a focusing hood (like an old Praktica camera), or a re-

versing prism (Ricoh TLS 401).

The construction as outlined above always works. The required projection distance of 12.5 cm (4.9 in.) is easily reached with intermediate rings and extension tubes, as illustrated in the photo on the left. Magnification is the same as that of the microscope. With a normal eyepiece, on the other hand, the enlargement is only half of the microscope enlargement.

Special Microscope Attachments

Some cameras come with their own specialized attachments for photomicrography, with longer tubes. These are very robust, practical, and affordable—for instance, the one from Olympus. However, you cannot change the degree

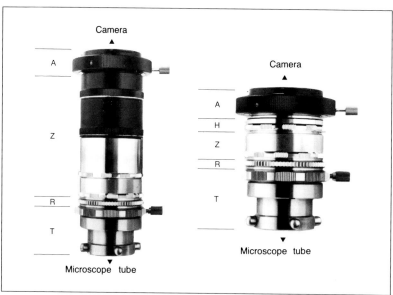

Example of how photomicrography attachments for a 35-mm camera are connected: Left: typical sequence. Right: with image field lens (Göke).
T = microscope tube adapter
R = intermediate dovetail ring attachment
Z = M-42 extension tube
H = auxiliary lens in an M-42 ring
A = adapter

of magnification because the tube cannot be extended.

If you want to view and photograph a larger portion of an image, you can use fewer intermediate rings than mentioned in the above-outlined system, accepting a slight decrease in the quality of the picture. The danger of vignetting can be avoided by using a wide-angle eyepiece. Of course, this won't work when individual attachments have been added; however, the disadvantages are not very serious when working with standard magnification.

Wide-Field Photography

A camera can usually see only part of what your eyes see. If you want to extend the projected image as far to the margins as possible, you might want to consider an auxiliary lens (for instance the F-201 from Göke). This lens is connected to the camera at the adapter, using only one (short) intermediate ring (see the right photo, page 60). The trick here is a reduction of the so-called "transfer" factor.

The advantage of this arrangement is that the length of the unit is much shorter, which gives the whole system more stability. However, since a much larger section of the viewing field is projected onto the 35-mm format, the overall magnification is reduced. When using an F-201 lens and a smaller intermediate ring, the "camera factor" is about 0.3 and magnification on the negative is therefore $0.3 \times$ the total magnification (as dis-

cussed on page 27). Eyepieces lower than $10 \times$ will, however, show some vignetting. If the eyepiece magnification is even smaller, the total viewing field on the negative looks like a spherical disk, which on occasion might be just what we want.

Focusing

Focusing is indeed a tricky business. The range-finder and microprism screen of the camera won't work. Rough-grained ground glass does not show details. What works best is uniformly fine-grained ground glass, as is used in cameras with exchangeable ground glass screens (for instance, the Olympus) to take pictures with high-powered teleobjectives.

But here, too, focusing is not easy. However, there is a way out: find the point when there is the least amount of blurring, which means moving the adjustment knob *swiftly* to and fro in decreasing sweeps, until you end up somewhere "in the middle" between the two extreme positions (tube a bit too far up and tube a bit too far down). A clear glass focusing screen with cross hairs is also available. As a rule, it works similarly to an eyepiece with boundary lines in a trinocular tube, which can be attached to the eyepiece support. Proceed as follows: (1) With relaxed eyes, focus on the cross hairs of the photomask (on the camera, turn the *viewer* of the right-angle viewfinder; on the eyepiece of the microscope, the eyelens). (2) Focus on the

Olympus OM 2 N 35-mm reflex camera with cable release (attached at the factory).

specimen by lowering and raising the tube, again with a relaxed eyes. (Look up at an object some yards [meters] away and then look quickly into the microscope. Crosshairs or demarcation lines should be sharp then.) This process works quite well for more powerful magnification. For low-power magnification (particularly when one has little experience or isn't concentrating), the image may be out of focus, even if you have been absolutely convinced that the microscopic image in the binocular or on the clear glass was focused. If you don't improve after a few trials, use a ground-glass instead of clear glass focusing screen.

Fast-moving microorganisms cannot be photographed satisfactorily without a trinocular tube (and a microflash attachment; see page 64). Look through the binocular and find the subject in the field of view. Choose a subject that is located in the center of the field and provides good contrast, and bring it into sharp focus. Then make sure that the subject is in the center of the camera's viewfinder and also is in focus. If the subject is not in sharp focus in the camera's viewfinder, you might have to adjust the distance between the camera and the microscope by adding the proper connecting rings or by adjusting the eyepiece. If possible, move the lens facing the camera in slow motion back and forth until the image is in focus; if that isn't possible, raise the eyepiece slightly, measure the distance, and have a ring made for you that can then be slipped over the eyepiece to keep it in the appropriate position relative to the upper end of the tube. If this process has been properly carried out (some camera systems have already been adjusted at the factory), the problem of proper focusing can be laid to rest. Whatever your eye sees clearly, your camera does also. However, I

recommend that you check for accuracy each time you start a new film and, if necessary, make the proper adjustments.

Proper exposure

In the past, choosing proper exposure was one of the main problems. Hundreds of suggestions were made, scores of manufacturers were recommended. But today, with the invention of the built-in Cd-exposure meter, the problem of using the right exposure for a given job has lost much of its horror. In the past, proper exposure was measured with a light meter (on which a pointer adjusted to a particular mark), a process that required you to take frequent sample photographs to check for accuracy. Modern light meters (preferably those that allow for longer exposure, maybe 10–20 seconds) have by now solved almost all of these problems. For that reason I recommend, very simply, nothing less than a good shutter mechanism with a camera mirror that can be locked up before taking a picture, and so create as little vibration as possible. However, even these systems need to have test photographs taken and occasionally need to be recalibrated.

In order to get the best results, depending on the specimen, the automatic mechanism is deliberately set to either underexpose (darkfield with only a few bright details) or overexpose (brightfield with a few dark details), either ½ or one aperture stops

(f-stops) each time. When in doubt, it might pay off to bracket your exposures: "proper exposure"; "proper exposure plus ½ f-stop"; "proper exposure minus ½ f-stop."

Vibration

It is inevitable the mirror of a 35-mm reflex camera will cause vibrations as it moves up when the picture is taken, particularly when the attachments make the whole assembly rather tall and extreme magnification is attempted. Even when the stand of the microscope is heavy (and very expensive), photomicrographs can be hopelessly blurred. We do have several remedies:

1. Fold the mirror up before taking the picture, using the mirror lock-up feature. (This, however, is possible on only a few cameras.)

2. Avoid "dangerous" exposure times, for instance $\frac{1}{50}$ second to 1 second (the worst is $\frac{1}{5}$ second), altogether. In other words, use very short exposure times ($\frac{1}{100}$ second or even shorter than that) or very long exposure times (longer than 1 or 2 seconds). In the latter case, the vibration won't have any effect because by the time the total exposure takes place the vibration of the equipment has already been dissipated.

3. Use microflash attachments where illumination time, and thereby exposure, is automatically adjusted by the camera (see page 64).

4. With the Olympus OM 2

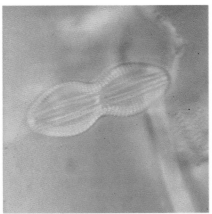

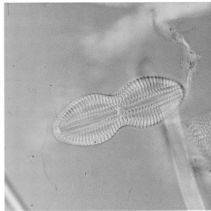

Left: Diatoms (*Diploneis* spec.) taken with ⅕ second exposure; in spite of the fact that the microscope is set on a heavy base, the photo is blurred. Right: same subject, taken with the "cardboard method" (see text), is impeccably sharp.

camera, every vibration is avoided due to its special off-the-film metering exposure system; it allows you to make use of a very elegant procedure (when the subject is static): Set the camera on "auto," turn off the light source, and release the shutter. The shutter opens and remains open. After about 1 or 2 seconds, turn the light back on via an extension switch. As soon as the film has received sufficient light, the shutter will close automatically. The Olympus OM 2 is not sold anymore; however, you might be able to purchase a used one. In my opinion, there is still nothing better than the old OM 2.

Some color distortions are possible with the latter method when shorter exposure times are used because, while the bulb warms up, the light has a reddish hue. Instead of turning the light on and off, there is a very simple way of screening and unscreening the light. Take a piece of cardboard and slide it over the light source. Then release the shutter and remove the cardboard from the light source. All photos in this book that were taken without a flash were done by this "cardboard method."

Shutter release and film advance

If you have ever tried to photograph at high magnification with an extremely tall camera setup, advancing the film via a quick gear-shift mechanism, you will want to send the whole system to the devil, believe me. For photomicrography, the answer to our prayers is the automatic film advance or *winder*. Nothing needs to be adjusted, and all vibrations created when the film is advanced have dissipated after about ⅕ to ½ second. Furthermore, the shutter can be released with an electric switch via a cable release. If necessary, you can make yourself a foot switch where you can take a whole series of pictures (2 per second with a winder, 5 per second with a motorized drive), and always have one hand free to operate the mechanical stage and the other hand to operate the focusing mechanism. In this way, you won't miss those once-in-a-lifetime shots, where the opportunity is usually gone in a few seconds.

Micro-flash

Micro-flash is recommended for two reasons:

1. The danger of blurring is eliminated once and for all, provided that you have used a computerized micro-flash.

2. The color quality of the electronic flash allows you to use very affordable daylight reversal color film without or almost always without using a filter.

63

You will never use anything else once you have worked with such a flash. However, there are only very few (very expensive) micro-flash attachments on the market. But if you are handy you can put together a very functional system yourself.

Two Optically Accurate Possibilities

There are two possibilities:

1. Position the filaments of the flash (strobe) and the low voltage lamp so that both are imaged onto the condenser diaphragm. When the flash occurs, the light will follow the path for good

Köhler illumination.

2. With the help of a piece of glass or a semipermeable mirror, the flash is "mirrored" into the illumination path so that both come together and create one single image in the condenser diaphragm plane, as described under 1.

Two different solutions are possible with semipermeable (partially silvered) mirrors. If you have enough room, add a beam-splitter plate at a 45° angle between the bulb and the condenser lens (as shown in Choice a of the figure). If this is not possible, place the mir-

Base-mounted illumination system from Zeiss (see page 43) that was expanded into a micro-flash by adding a flash tube with an intermediate optic.

ror in front of the photomicrographic diaphragm (see Choice b). The latter is the system I prefer to use. It is an Olympus flash system, where the automatic control shuts off the flash at the proper moment: a fully automated flash illumination (off-the-film metering). The flash is mounted on a structure made from a compound board. The space needed for the lamp tube was cut out and a semipermeable mirror was mounted at a 45° angle, allowing about 20% transmitted illu-

Filament · Collector lens · Illuminated field diaphragm · Aperture diaphragm · condenser · Objective · Specimen plane · flash bulb · Choice a · Choice b · flash bulb

Above: Diagram of Köhler illumination. Below: two choices for light reflection with Köhler illumination (see text).

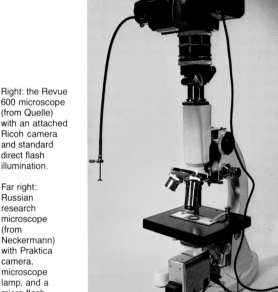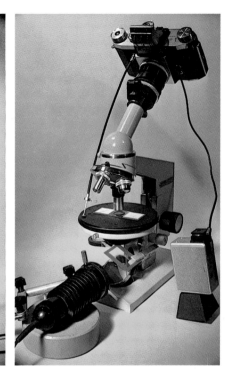

Right: the Revue 600 microscope (from Quelle) with an attached Ricoh camera and standard direct flash illumination.

Far right: Russian research microscope (from Neckermann) with Praktica camera, microscope lamp, and a micro-flash system arranged over a slide.

mination from the light bulb and 80% from the reflected flash. The ray path isn't altogether correct, but is sufficient for most purposes.

Useful Improvisations

In addition to these two rather cumbersome choices for combining a microscope and flash attachment, I want to show you two more that are much simpler:

1. Arrange a flash (possibly with a diffusing screen if the flash is too bright or uneven) on a small table stand in such a way that the flash is directed upward (where possible, folding the reflec-

tor back approximately 90°) and, with the adjustment completed, move the stand directly under the condenser.

Of course, the normal illuminator is now covered up and you must choose between either viewing the image or taking the photo (left photo).

2. Arrange a glass plate at a 45° angle between the exit point of the light in the base of the microscope and the condenser, and adjust the flash. About 7% of the light from the flash will come through, which is sufficient when you use a strong flash

and a low-power objective (right photo).

Partially mirrored glass surfaces are, of course, better. You can make one yourself by removing most of the coating from the back of a simple pocket mirror with sandpaper until only a fine layer of the silver coating is left.

The correct film

Color Film

Here, everybody has a favorite and some swear that only theirs is the proper choice. The scientist will match the spectral sensitivity of the chosen film to that of the spectral

65

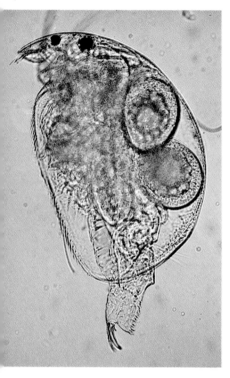

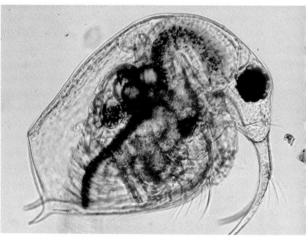

Left: Sharply detailed photo of *Alona costata* taken with flash; exposure time approximately 1/5000 second (a darkfield photograph of the embryo is shown on page 50).

Above: Water flea *Bosmina longirostris*; exposure time 1/250 second; the "foot," caught in the process of stretching out, is blurred.

output of the light source and the dominant colors in the object to be photographed. The amateur is best advised to simply try a few different kinds of film and stay with the one that is most pleasing.

With a blue filter (see page 67), it is possible to change the color quality of the lamp in such a way that you can work with daylight color-reversal film, which is available practically everywhere and also usually is the least expensive. Besides, daylight color-reversal film is the proper choice when using an electronic flash.

In addition, I recommend the use of slide film only, letting an expert use color negative film. Today it is possible to have photos made from slides that are of good quality and inexpensive; also, duplicate slides can easily be made from the original. With the help of an intermediate negative, it is possible to produce black-and-white enlargements from a slide.

Black-and-White Film

Since a microscopic object, compared to those in our natural environment, has relatively poor contrast, I recommend that you use in general a low-speed film with high contrast (to be developed with "high gamma"). Generally speaking, however, I prefer to use ISO 100/21° film that is subsequently developed normally or with increased contrast, depending on the preparations. An exception is the low-speed film for documentation of approximately ISO 6/10°. Do not hesitate to reach for such a film if you take a lot of pictures for the purpose of comparing specimens that have particularly sharp details but where, by nature, contrast might be poor; these films come in 10 m rolls and are inexpensive. The choice of specific filters may be very important in black-and-white photography, as is explained in the following pages.

Instant Film

It is also possible to attach a Polaroid camera, or a camera with a Polaroid back, to a microscope. For the purpose of research and in criminology this is often the method of choice, but, generally speaking, I only recommend the use of instant photography when you want to check the quality of illumination, because on one hand this method is rather expensive, and on the other hand, by its very nature this type of film creates an awful lot of trash that has to be taken care of, something that we will have to pay much more attention to in the future.

Color filters

In Color Photography

Color filters can on one hand be used to eliminate color distortions; on the other hand, you can have a lot of fun by using filters for the opposite purpose: to create a photograph in which the background and specimen are in contrasting colors.

You must use a blue filter in order to accommodate a daylight film to incandescent illumination. Experiment with a few different filters ("conversion filters") that are available in photo stores and choose the one that gives the transpar-

ency the best color quality in your eyes. It's important not to judge the color quality while viewing the transparency against a reddish-tinted lamp or against a blue sky. Use a slide projector.

It is possible to give a picture an ocean-blue background—as is often desirable for photos of plankton—by using a more intensely colored blue filter (or two conversion filters together). Also, it is fun to create a "hydrobiological mood" with green-tinted filters. That is, however, a matter of taste. If carefully used, so-called "trendy photography" can sometimes elicit an admiring "ahhh" from the viewing audience during a slide presentation, but be very careful with such applications when producing transparencies for documentation.

In Black-and-White Photography

It is really amazing what drastic changes using a colored filter can make in the contrast of colored specimens with their backgrounds when you use black-and-white film. A basic rule is: A color filter makes those parts of an object that are the same color as the filter lighter in black-and-white prints, while the complementary color becomes darker.

Every amateur photographer knows that a yellow filter makes a blue sky in a black-and-white enlargement darker; blue is the complementary color of yellow. The more intense the color of the filter, the greater the effect. The four color filters most often used give you the following effects:

Blue filter: red and yellowish tints turn darker; blue tints become lighter.

Green filter: pink tints turn darker; green tints become lighter.

Yellow filter: blue-violet tints turn darker; yellow tints become lighter.

Red filter: blue tints turn darker; red tints become lighter.

Microscopy specimens are usually stained in contrasting colors, meaning they are stained in 2 or 3 different colors that selectively give a specific color to different parts of a cell. The stains chosen should be sufficiently different—for instance, blue

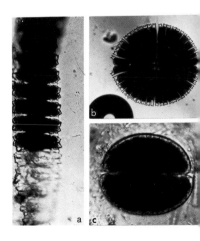

Black-colored chromatophores of a green algae (desmid), photographed with a deep red filter. a: Genus *Desmidium* (lower portion is dead). b: Genus *Micrasterias*. c: Genus *Cosmarium*.

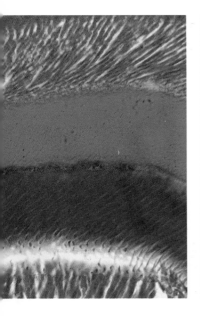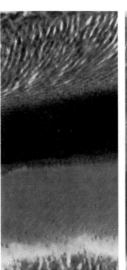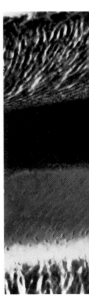

Cross-section of the layers of a mammalian tooth. The far-left cross-section is stained with azan. From top to bottom: enamel-building tissue and enamel (red); dentine (blue); tooth-building tissue.

At right: the same specimen, photographed in black-and-white with three different color filters: left, blue filter; middle, red filter; right, green filter. Note how the filters work. The blue filter turns the red-dyed enamel much darker; with a red filter it becomes so light that even very delicate internal structures become visible. The green filter turns the enamel into a deep black color, but differentiates the remaining tissues too, thus creating very good contrasts.

and red. A double-stain using haematoxylin–eosin will color the nucleus blue and cell's plasma, muscle cells, and connective tissue more or less red. Trichrome staining was developed by Masson and modified by Goldner. Here the cell nucleus becomes dark brown, cell plasma, muscle tissue and red blood cells become red, and connective tissue and cartilage become green (see the photo on page 103).

For a black-and-white photo of a specimen stained with haematoxylin–eosin, if you want to make the blue cell nucleus even darker and really contrast it with the rest of the image, use a red filter. If, on the other hand, you would like to emphasize the yellowish-red surroundings, to make the cell plasma and muscle tissue darker, use a blue filter. A generally contrast-rich photograph can be obtained by using a green or yellowish-green filter; red becomes relatively dark, but blue also comes out very satisfactorily.

Examples of the Use of Filters

In microscopic specimens counterstained with eosin, we usually try to increase the contrast of the delicate red tones by using green filters.

- When the main interest is emphasizing the green chromatophores, use deep red filters, which will make them appear black (see photos on page 67) (however, this diminishes resolution when a high-power objective is used).

- If you want to make the best use of an achromat, use a yellowish green filter; for colorless objects, like diatoms and radiolarian shells, use a dark green filter. The reason for improvements in the quality of the photograph taken with a yellowish green filter becomes apparent when you remember that the achromat is corrected in only one of three spectral areas (see page 29). The process of filtering eliminates the most bothersome spectral shifts, so that they won't be visible in the negative.

Other Filters. Many other filters are available, like neutral-density filters (recommended for reducing luminosity without affecting the spectral composition of the light); heat-absorption filters, highly recommended with high-power illumination and when the iris of the condenser diaphragm is wide open; as well as color compensating filters, used in special cases.

High-contrast photomicrography

There are several ways of making reproductions from photomicrographs that look almost like drawings. Take the pictures using a high-contrast, low-sensitivity film that is developed to maximize the contrast. Here, the exposure is critical and must be exact; I recommend using a calibrated automatic timer.

The enlargements are made on high-contrast paper and have very few grey tones. Make xerographic copies of the enlargements using a well-adjusted xerographic copier. This will eliminate the rest of the grey tones, producing in the end a high-contrast illustration that will look like a drawing.

Xerographic copying works so well that you even can use regular photographs that have been processed on lower-contrast paper (see photos above). The only thing that needs to be mentioned here is that one ought to work, if possible, with parallel illumination, which reproduces even

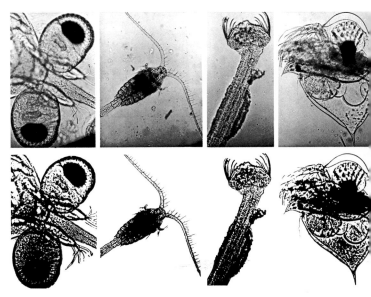

Marine plankton. From left to right: head of a larval crustacean; copepod, chaetognath, and waterflea. Top row: Photomicrographs using a rather low-contrast film and a poorly adjusted (eccentric) illuminated field diaphragm. Achromat, 10 ×; no eyepiece, no condenser. Below: high-contrast "double" xerographic copies. The remaining shadows were removed with white correction fluid.

The photos in the second row were made to look like line drawings, which is the preferred method for presenting specimens in scientific publications because they are much less expensive than halftones. The photos in the top row had to be printed in as halftones.

Left: Photomicrographs of marine diatom *Biddulphia*, made under very simple conditions. Right: Double xerographic copy.

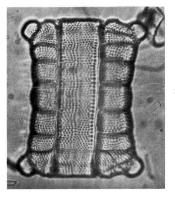 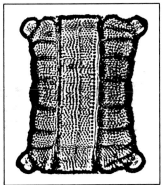

Video camera, attached to the Laborlux microscope from Leica (formerly, Leitz). The camera (by itself very light) is held in place by a copy stand from Kaiser. For focusing, I recommend a video monitor rather than a viewfinder.

the most delicate structures with sharp contours. In these cases I use a low-power objective without the condenser. The photos on the bottom right (page 69) are of a marine

diatom, photographed once with standard optics and a low-cost plug-in illuminator; to its right is the result of xerocopying the photograph and then xerocopying the first xerocopy again. Such a hard-contoured "double" copy looks like an ink drawing. Details are slightly distorted, but that would be the case in an ink drawing as well.

Film and videotape

Film Camera

A super-8 film camera, one in which the lenses are either removed or focused on infinity, can be mounted just like a 35-mm camera or—better yet—attached to a copy stand and adjusted to the microscope. Move as far toward the eye lens of the photo eyepiece as possible until the image in the viewfinder is not vignetting anymore.

The main problem is the vibration created by the motor of the camera. Even though the motor of a modern film camera runs quietly and smoothly, minute vibrations—particularly when you are working at high-power magnification—are very bothersome. For that reason I do not recommend attaching the camera directly to the microscope, because from $100 \times$ magnification on, the viewing field begins to vibrate. If you have bad luck, that may even happen with $20 \times$ magnification. If you use super-8 extensively, or you are perhaps even thinking of producing 16-mm films, it is essential that you

build a wall console. Use a heavy chip board and make the height adjustable. The connection between the camera arm and the eyepiece tube can be made lightproof with a bellows.

For the amateur, however, a video camera is the camera of choice. The advantages are obvious: no vibrations, inexpensive videotape, and you can immediately view the results.

Camcorder

Using the camcorder is simple: mount the camcorder vertically on the copy stand, and position the microscope underneath it, and make sure that the connection is lightproof. The problem of vibrations when the camera is running does not exist. Viewing and focusing take place either with the horizontally turned viewfinder or, better yet, via a connected TV screen. The camcorder sensor should meet the intermediate image; so remove the eyepiece and part of the upper tube.

A camcorder without removable lenses is a bit more problematic. Here, position the camcorder lens at infinity, move as close to the eyepiece as possible and use a wide-angle eyepiece.

There are practically no limits when using a video system. If the specimen or section is static, a certain dynamic drive can be created by moving the stage; even zoom oculars can be used. Slow-motion shots of rapidly moving organisms and time-lapse photography, in the case of slow-moving protozoa or subjects with similar characteristics, have been more easily made with conventional film cameras. However, some video recorders now have security time lapse possibilities also (e.g., Panasonic).

Video Printer

If you own a video printer, you might do well to think of switching to a video system for your microscopy documentation. Such printed images are much more expensive than conventional paper enlargements and do not have the power of resolution and depth of color of photography (the latter is particularly true when compared to slides). However, printing your video film does have invaluable advantages. Contrast is much better when using a high-resolution process, maybe S-VHS or Hi-8. The other advantages are as follows:

1. The camcorder can run for a longer period. You only print those pictures that are of interest to you, leaving out others that you don't like.

2. Contrast and depth of color can be modified.

3. Several pictures can be combined as a series on a single print.

4. The results can be checked immediately.

5. High sensitivity of the camcorder allows you to work with very short exposure times, like $1/1000$ second or less, so the video pictures will look like flash photos. With higher-power illumination, it is possible to use exposure times of $1/10000$ second!

6. Some video recorders screen not only full-frame pictures (25 pictures per second) but also half-frame pictures. With somewhat diminished power of resolution, one can thus create a slight time-lapse effect (50 pictures per second).

Diatoms. On the left (top to bottom): *Surirella spiralis,* with focus on different depths. On the right: ribbed diatom, *Pinnularia* spec. shell in lateral and midline views. Above: normal photomicrograph. Below: video pictures taken at the same time via a beam splitter using half-frame screening (see text), printed in black-and-white (Mitsubishi printer) and displayed in a series.

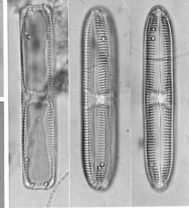

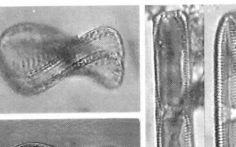
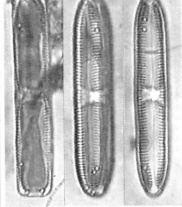

DRAWING AND MEASURING

Why make drawings?

The most important reason for making microscopy drawings is to create simple outlines that, for instance, allow you to map out the length–width relations of a specimen. When those dimensions are correct, no special drawing equipment is needed to quickly add life to a drawing with a few lines. However, make sure that your artistic ambitions don't run away with you—don't try to add shadows and other decorations. Stay with the simple outlines of the contours and the proper recording of organs, cell contents, etc. (see examples on page 74). Differences in density or spatial curvature can be indicated by drawing dense or less dense stippling.

To make a drawing, use a medium-hard pencil and strong, smooth drawing paper. Adding ink or watercolor is somewhat problematic, but possible (the drawing on page 74 is a good example). Microscopy drawing, although not very popular, has two huge advantages over even the most wonderful photomicrographs:

- With the aid of the micrometer screw of the microscope, it is possible to "optically

An improvised drawing setup with high-intensity illumination, an obliquely positioned small microscope, and an auxiliary prism. A paper shield between objective and slide reduces glare.

scan" several layers of an image, transferring to the paper a clear composite picture of what are often spatially very confusing structures.

- You can make an abstraction of an image, freeing it from sometimes bothersome non-essential details.

This process makes it possible to refine one ideal drawing from several different and not very satisfactory specimens.

A good drawing is always the end product of an extensive process of observation and transfer. Making accurate three-dimensional drawings of extensive structures (for instance, radiolarian skeletons) requires practice and good spatial sense. The drawing on top of page 74 was made by an experienced architect who is also very interested in biology.

Drawing without additional equipment

It is possible to draw without the aid of any additional accessories. If you are right-handed look into a monocular tube with your left eye; with your right eye, look at the tip of the pencil on a piece of paper next to the microscope. (Left-handed people should reverse this arrangement.) With a bit of concentration, your brain will blend the images from both eyes; the tip of the pencil, moving on the paper, will outline the contour.

Drawing accessories

With a drawing eyepiece (camera lucida), it is possible to

bring the drawing paper, placed to the right of the microscope, into the field of view. In the past, every well-known manufacturer made these eyepieces. The tip of the pencil is visible in the field of vision, transferring the outline of the contours to the paper. The disadvantage of this procedure is that the drawing board must be laterally placed because of the oblique path of rays in the drawing eyepiece.

Such a disadvantage has been eliminated with the aid of

Drawing eyepiece with auxiliary mirror from Hertel & Reuss.

Inexpensive projection attachment from Hertel & Reuss.

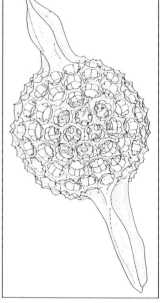

Photographs of a radiolarian under Köhler illumination with condenser diaphragm reduced to ⅔. Left: focusing on the largest diameter. Right: focusing on the upper portion. Drawing, right: Reconstruction, based on the photos shown and others. (Drawing by B. Kresling.)

Below: Example of well-done, simple ink drawings of microscopic specimens (from Meyer and Lieder, *Begleitbuch zu Mikroskopischen Präparaten und Microdias*, J. Lieder Co., Ludwigsburg, Germany).

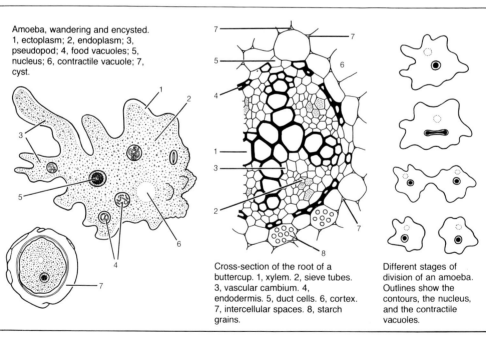

Amoeba, wandering and encysted. 1, ectoplasm; 2, endoplasm; 3, pseudopod; 4, food vacuoles; 5, nucleus; 6, contractile vacuole; 7, cyst.

Cross-section of the root of a buttercup. 1, xylem. 2, sieve tubes. 3, vascular cambium. 4, endodermis. 5, duct cells. 6, cortex. 7, intercellular spaces. 8, starch grains.

Different stages of division of an amoeba. Outlines show the contours, the nucleus, and the contractile vacuoles.

a drawing apparatus that has a laterally mounted deflecting mirror, or with a more modern drawing apparatus such as the one from Olympus; here, prisms contained in a laterally extended, long tube project the image distortion-free onto the horizontally positioned drawing paper.

A very simple method uses a deflecting mirror or a deflecting prism on an eyepiece. In a darkened room, an image is projected onto a piece of drawing paper (see photo, page 72).

Drawing apparatus with integrated deflecting prism from Olympus.

Identifying the amount of magnification of a negative

For scientific purposes it is imperative that we know the correct size of the overall magnification. One could, of course, simply go by the formula: *Total magnification = objective magnification × eyepiece magnification*. But this does not hold true for standard camera attachments.

Here is the way to arrive at the correct information: make a photograph of the stage micrometer, which is a 1-mm scale mounted on a glass microscope slide. This scale is divided, for instance, 1 mm into 100 segments, or 2 mm into 200 segments. The distance between each segment is $\frac{1}{100}$ mm or 10μm (1 μm equals

one-thousandth of a millimeter), and $\frac{1}{20}$ of a millimeter is indicated by a mark longer than the rest of the marks on the micrometer's scale. After the film is developed, measure the negative with a ruler. If, for instance $\frac{2}{10}$ mm when photographed measures 3.10 cm, you know that magnification on the negative is
31 mm: .2 mm = 155.

Measuring with an eyepiece micrometer

First, you must calibrate the eyepiece micrometer (a glass disk etched with a $\frac{1}{10}$ mm scale, placed in the eyepiece over the visual field diaphragm). Place a stage micrometer on the microscope and rotate the eyepiece until the two scales are parallel. Move the stage micrometer until one of the left scale lines matches up with a scale line of the eyepiece micrometer (see drawing at right). Look to the right side of the field of view and find where the scale of the stage micrometer again matches up exactly with the scale marker of the eyepiece micrometer. In the upper portion of the picture, for example, the left edge of the 4 and the 15 marks of the stage micrometer (thick lines) line up with the 19 and the 84 marks of the eyepiece micrometer (thin lines). The number of eyepiece micrometer scale divisions (84 − 19 = 65) corresponds to the actual distance, the number of stage micrometer scale divisions (15 − 4 =

11). Since each division of the stage micrometer is $\frac{1}{100}$ mm or 10μm, the actual distance is number of divisions times 10μm (11 × 10μm = 110μm). Since it takes 65 eyepiece divisions to cover the same distance, you divide the actual distance covered (110μm) by 65. Therefore, 1 eyepiece micrometer division is equal to 1.69μm. After the chosen objective–eyepiece combination has been calibrated, measurements are simple. For instance, look at the two fibers below (grey strips in the lower part of the illustration), and you will see that, according to the illustration, they cover 16 − 4 = 12 and 94 − 82 = 12 eyepiece micrometer spaces, so the fiber thickness is 12 × 1.69μm = 20.3μm. Rounded out, the thickness of a fiber is 20μm.

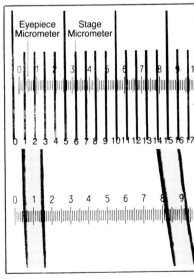

Example of calibration and measuring (see text).

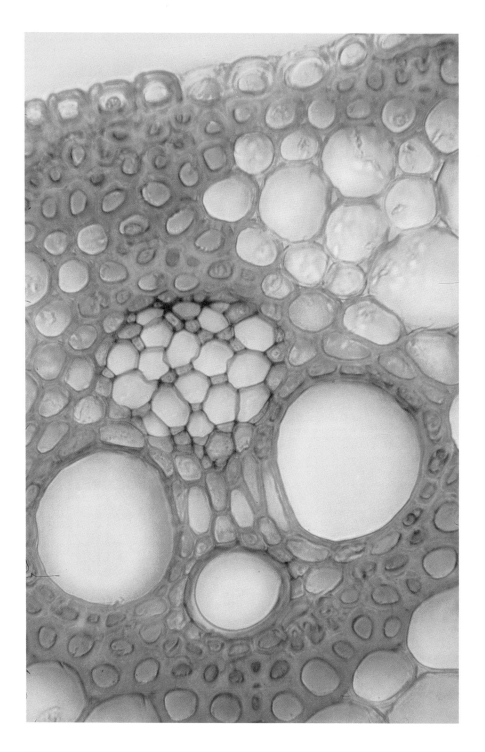

THE WORLD OF PLANTS

The hunting grounds

What Is Worth Collecting?

Many plants grow in freshwater; in some places they are more numerous than the flowering plants that grow on land. As far as numbers are concerned, freshwater algae are always good to pursue, a subject discussed in the chapter on aquatic organisms beginning on page 110. As far as fungi are concerned, molds are easy to prepare and are preferable to a cross-section of a mushroom. Reindeer moss is very good for studying reproductive organs. Mosses are very beautiful and are interesting to examine, especially their small leaves and reproductive organs. The sporangia of the fern are also very interesting.

Seed-bearing plants offer many possibilities: the surfaces of leaves, cross-sections of leaves, thin stems and roots, or various cross-sections of wood. A razor blade glued to a piece of wood, or a straight razor, may replace a microtome for making cross-sections. The specimen to be cut can be held fast between the halves of the split pith of an elder bush branch.

Many specimens are available for microscopic examina-

Stained cross-section of a corn stem. The large tubelike structures transport water or sap.

tion. From a piece of onion skin to demonstrate cell structures all the way to the filament hair of the *Tradescantia*, which demonstrates plasma flow, all are worthy of investigation.

Studying Plant Development

Everything that is alive and grows is interesting, because structures within an organism change all the time. For instance, one can make cuts through a germinating rye seed, beginning with the first delicate shoot, all the way to a wilted or dead stem. The development of leaves also is interesting, from the leaf bud all the way until it unfolds; try longitudinal sections, viewed with incident illumination. It is also very exciting to watch the development and formation of a fruit, starting with ovaries (longitudinal and cross-sections) and continuing with flowers and then ripened fruit. Stone fruits (drupes) are good choices for such a study.

Cutting specimens

Using a Razor Blade

Very delicate parts of a plant are best prepared by wedging them into the pith of an elder bush branch that was pulled off the bush in the fall. The pith is cleft lengthwise. Hold the pith in the left hand, after having tied it together with twine so that the wedge does not come out. With the hand resting comfortably on the table, cut the specimen horizontally in a pulling rather than pushing motion. It won't take long for you to get the right

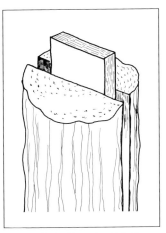

A piece of a leaf is wedged into the pith of an elder bush branch.

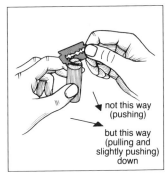

not this way (pushing)

but this way (pulling and slightly pushing) down

Holding the razor blade while cutting a wedged-in specimen.

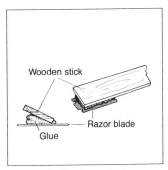

Wooden stick

Razor blade

Glue

An example of an improvised microtome knife, which is easy to make.

combination of pressure and speed of motion. With this simple method it will be easy to produce a specimen 1 to 2 cell layers thick for examination. It does not have to be thinner than that. If you don't want to hold the razor blade in your fingers, you might want to glue it to a piece of wood (see drawing on p. 77, bottom). Hold the blade parallel to the cutting surface when cutting.

Using a Handheld Microtome and Razor

If you intend to make many plant cuttings, you might do well to purchase a small handheld microtome, which can be purchased inexpensively. You

How to use the hand-held microtome.

Cross-section of a bean embryo. In the cells, reserve material and crystals are easily seen; the cut was made from fresh material by hand with the razor-blade technique we have been discussing.

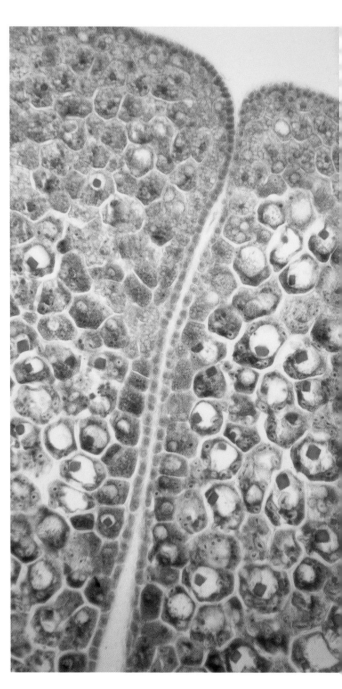

78

may also choose between simple table microtomes and those that are particularly heavy, which you do not have to hold down when making your cut. Both have glass tops used to guide the knife—again, it is more a pulling than pushing motion. By turning a centrally located, very delicate screw, it is possible to make sections no thicker than $\frac{1}{100}$ mm.

The cutting edge of the razor must always be in perfect condition, but sharpening itself is an art form that one can seldom master to perfection. It is far better and easier to invest a few dollars and send the knife to an expert shop for sharpening. Knives used in barber shops are not recommended; rather purchase one in a specialty shop.

Microthek has brought a small and inexpensive table microtome on the market that allows you to attach a razor blade. This is very practical, because whenever a blade gets dull, you just need to change the blade.

Using a Craft Knife

Instead of using an expensive microtome, one can easily use a craft knife (the topmost portion, when dull, may be snapped off). Craft knives are inexpensive and are easily found in hobby shops. It is best to use the blade without the handle so that you can hold it at an angle, as the blade slides over the cutting surface. It is very important that you pull rather than push the blade.

If you come across some plant sections that are difficult to cut, you might want to harden them first. Immerse them for 2 to 3 weeks in methylated spirits. You can also moisten the blade with the same spirits.

I do not recommend creating permanent slides; it is much more satisfying to go on an excursion with your handheld microtome, cut a cross-section from whatever catches your fancy, examine it in a drop of water when it is still fresh, and compare it to the illustration and discussion in a botanical histology textbook.

This might also give you some more ideas for further experiments; there truly is a whole world that one can explore, and none of it is difficult.

The cut edges of hand-cut samples are particularly interesting, because they are the thinnest part; with delicate angled cuts, they can be as thin as $\frac{1}{1000}$ mm.

Permanent slides

Some companies make permanent slides that are expertly prepared, perfectly stained, extremely thin, safely embedded, and they cost very little. What more can anyone possibly want?

When I began discovering the plant kingdom, while I was still a student, I always worked in two ways. I would collect interesting biological specimens, for instance a pine needle, make numerous cross-sections in every conceivable direction

Green-filtered photograph of a cross-section of a *Clematis vitalba* shoot. Diaphragm quite closed down to increase contrast. This slide was stored vertically, which caused the mounting medium to run out and be replaced by air bubbles; therefore, be careful and always store such slides horizontally.

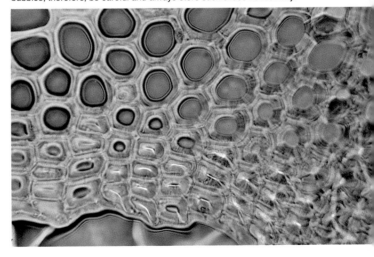

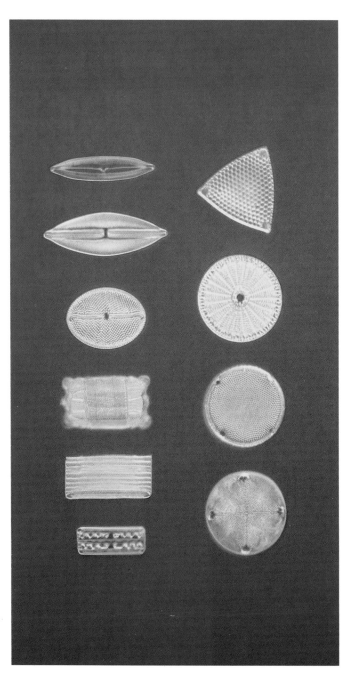

at every angle, and at the end of the session I would examine them thoroughly. And then, as a kind of reward, I would spend some money on a permanent, stained specimen. I studied my own specimens only when they were fresh. I do not think it is a good investment in time and effort to make your own (probably imperfect) permanent slides. The only permanent slides that I can recommend with good conscience that students make themselves are of diatoms.

Diatom specimens

Diatoms are microscopic one-celled plants that are found in the sea, lakes, ponds, streams, and on moist rocks, soil, or damp bark. Spring is the time when diatoms can be found in great masses as brown coverings on rocks, and on plants in ditches. Collect these in a small container, shake vigorously, and then let them sit for a while. After a day or so the diatoms have floated up to the surface in a fine brown layer. Transfer a small amount from this layer to a glass slide with a pipet, after discarding the first sample, because it still contains some sand. The drop on the glass disk is spread out and allowed to dry completely in

Arranged diatom collection, photographed under Rheinberg illumination; a doubled layer of blue foil was used to create a deep-blue background.

an oven at 100°C (212°F). Add a drop of mounting medium; if you wish, use a special diatom mounting medium (available in specialty stores) and cover it with a cover glass.

Cleaning the diatoms first will improve the quality of the product. Change the water repeatedly, allowing the contents to drift to the surface each time; delicate diatoms settle very slowly. Then hold the collected sediment in an old stainless steel spoon over a gas flame and thoroughly expose it to heat. The remaining white powder, the now-clean diatom shells, is then prepared for microscopic viewing as outlined above, after it has cooled off. The shells are now free of any organic substances, as well as the bothersome chromatophores; they truly look terrific. However, with this process (which we outlined only in rough form) it is almost impossible to avoid trapping air within the specimen.

In the past, the process of making a diatom slide was frequently done as follows: an eyelash, glued to a holder, was used to arrange the diatoms on a glass slide like little soldiers. Today, almost nobody uses this method. Old slides produced in this fashion display many different shapes and often are the most treasured part of a collection (see the sample on the opposite page).

Algae

Many different algae that you might come across and try to identify are discussed in the chapter on microorganisms living in water. You can also examine a flowerpot that has been kept moist and look at the surface for blue-green and green algae. If you live close by the shore, don't forget to collect brown seaweed and look at the delicate fibers or the flat covering, using transmitted light.

Fungi

Mold is a popular name for certain fungi. Here are few tips for examining such specimens (see also page 136). Mold is easily cultivated in a humid chamber. Fill a soup plate with 1 cm (⅜ in.) of water, and set an egg cup in the middle. Put your growth medium—for instance, a piece of bread—into the egg cup and cover it with a small transparent bowl. The moist atmosphere you have created is a perfect environment to grow mold. Examine the mold first under incident illumination and with low-power magnification; then look at the developing spores (for instance, of bread molds), scraping them together under transmitted light and somewhat stronger magnification. Permanent fungus slides are more easily purchased than made.

Pilobolus (see photo on page 57), is another exciting fungus to grow. Put a piece of fresh horse dung in an empty marmalade glass or, if you prefer, into a transparent plastic container with a lid. Put the container in the humid chamber. Almost by themselves, the fruiting bodies of the fungus begin to form. At the end of the swollen, club-shaped spo-

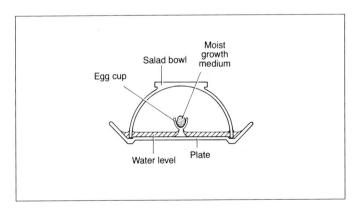

Example of a humid chamber made from kitchen utensils.

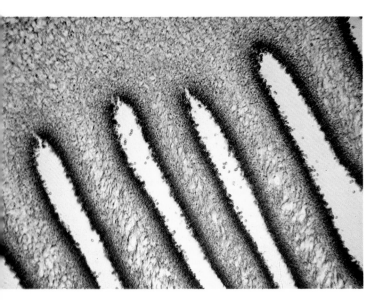

Cross-section of the cap of a mushroom (*Agaricus campester*) with lamellae and spores.

lichens, are particularly interesting. The nitrogen-loving yellow lichen *Parmelia acetabulum* is one example. Hose-shaped asci (spore sacs), with 8 spores each, are lined up like tin soldiers on its indented upper surface.

Bryophytes (mosses and liverworts)

Mosses and liverworts provide many opportunities for study. The sex organs are very interesting; however, they are not easy to find and are better purchased as permanent slides.

Many moss leaves are only a few cell layers thick. When they are suspended in a drop of water and pressed between the slide and cover glass, they are fascinating to watch: the

rangiophore, only a few millimeters in length is the long, dark sporangium, the size of the head of a pin, which is thrown by the plant with lightning speed toward the light. Seconds after having thrown off the sporangium, the sporangiophore collapses within itself.

Barberry leaves often carry rust-yellow swollen coverings that prove to be cup-shaped receptacles for spores. It is well-known that the barberry plant is the interim host of rust diseases. A botany book will give you more information on the particulars, and you can also find many other suggestions for specimens.

Lichens

Cross-sections of almost any type of lichen show the development of fungal hyphae and algae cells. Because of their relatively complex structures, the apothecia, key-shaped fruiting bodies of many tree

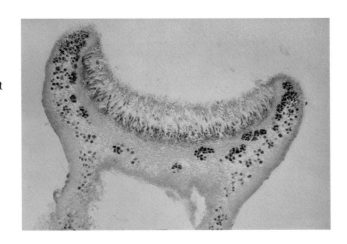

Cross-section of the fruiting body of a yellow lichen (*Parmelia acetabulum*).

cells, chloroplasts, and the flow of cytoplasm. When making a cross-section of the *thallus* of a liverwort, as the leaflike body is called (for instance, from the well-known brown liverwort *Marchantia*), you will find strange chimney-shaped structures (air pores) that are used for air exchange.

Sphagnum (peat moss) leaves are equally interesting. They have thin, live cells that contain chloroplasts and are imbedded in widely distributed, reinforced "water bags" (see photo to the right) with openings to the outside.

The leaf of the haircap moss (genus *Polytrichum*) is totally different. Here, the chlorophyll-carrying cells are arranged in closely-packed lamellae, as can be seen in a cross-section. The cap-covered capsule of a sporophyte is also worth looking at. After the cap has fallen off, the top of the capsule bursts open and shows a lineup of so-called *peristome teeth* at the edge of the opening. If the weather is damp, these little teeth curl toward the inside to prevent the spores from falling out.

Fern plants

Club mosses, horsetails, ferns, and water ferns all belong to the fern plants or Pterido-

Peristome teeth of a moss capsule. These "teeth" curl inside in response to humidity in the air.

View of a leaf of peat moss (*Sphagnum* spec.). The dead "water cells" are reinforced with ringlike structures, and the holes are for water intake. Rheinberg illumination, yellow against blue background.

phytes. (Today these ferns are often classified in three separate divisions.)

The sporangia, the spore capsules of the fern, are worth examining. They are only a few millimeters in size and usually sit in groups underneath a fine, round netlike structure on the underside of older leaves. When covered in a drop of water, they will burst open instantly, a process in which a caterpillar-shaped *annulus* (a ring of particularly strong cells) is involved.

If you make a horizontal cross-section of a moss leaf stem, you won't see many differentiated cells. When examining the stem of a fern, on the other hand, you will recognize definite vascular tissues in the center, and at the periphery, you will find supportive tissue, a first "division of labor."

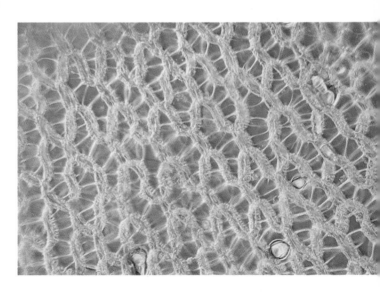

Seed-bearing plants

Naked-seed plants, or gymnosperms, including conifers, are interesting objects to study—for instance, their needles, young stems from just-germinated plants, and new shoots in season. Cross-sections are available as permanent slides in specialty shops. The indented stomates, resin channels, rings of hardened, thick cells surrounding them, and vascular structures imbedded in thin assimilation tissue are easily visible (see left photo). Cross-sections from woody plants can be studied to count the rings that represent annual growth.

Wood looks different depending on the cut: cuts can be made either horizontally, toward the center of the trunk/stem (radial), or along the length (tangential).

Among the covered-seed plants (angiosperms) very interesting cross-sections from leaves and stems can be made; but, here too, one will be hard put to work without a reliable instruction book and without—on occasion—the purchase of a permanent slide. As inspiration, a few tips are given below.

Section of a fern leaf (*Pterdium aquilinum*) with sporangium. The cohesion strength of the caterpillar-shaped outer ring (annulus) caused the spore capsule to burst. Rheinberg illumination.

Cross-section of a pine needle. Notice the thick epidermis with the indented stomata, the parenchyma (photosynthetic mesophyll) underneath, and the cross-section of the vascular bundles. The large, round areas are cross-sections through resin channels. Thin microtome cut.

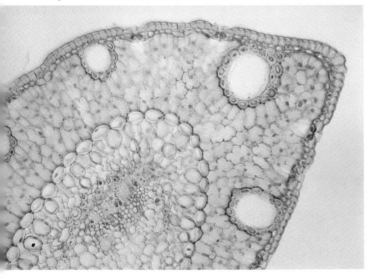

Leaf Surface

It is very interesting to observe the distribution of the stomates and the "folding" of the epidermis cells (cells that are on the surface of a leaf) under incident illumination or in bright transmitted light. A thin layer of the epidermis can be obtained either by a cut made parallel to the surface, or by peeling off a piece of the surface with a pair of tweezers. Transfer your sample to a glass slide, cover with a drop of water, and secure with a cover glass.

Leaf Print

Apply a few drops of a thin contact glue (or a few drops in turpentine) to the surface of a leaf. The dried glue skin will show an impression of the surface structure of the leaf. Put the dried glue layer between a slide and cover glass. For photos, use Rheinberg illumination.

Cross-Section of a Leaf

The variation in structures is endless. Beneath the protective surface layer (epidermis), where massive and more or less waterproof deposits can

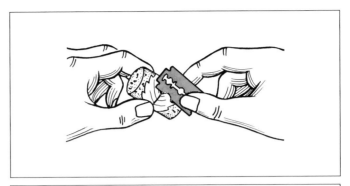

Top: surface cut from a leaf. Below: a layer of epidermis peeled off the surface of a leaf with tweezers.

A piece of epidermis of a leaf with stomates; condenser diaphragm almost closed.

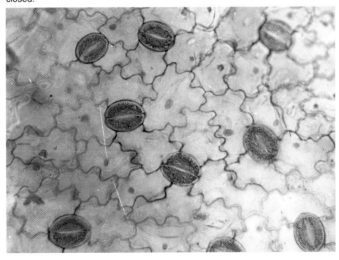

be seen, is the parenchyma, where the cells initially are closely packed, but with more of a meshlike, loose aggregation of cells underneath.

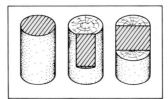

Illustration of three different possibilities (hatched lines) for cutting planes from plant shoots, stems, or twigs. From left to right: cross-section; tangential section; radial section.

it is very interesting to observe differences, morphologically as well as biochemically, in the arrangement of the strengthening fibers in young shoots and stems of different plants. Most of the time the stems are hollow and the supporting tissues are located as far to the outside as possible, increasing

thereby the stem's ability to support the plant. This can be seen in cross-sections of stems of the horsetail, stems of ordinary grass, and thousands of other examples.

Shoot Cross-Section

Cross-sections of conifers, deciduous trees, and foliage are very interesting, and the most easily obtained cross-sections are those from shoots. If plants are too mushy, put them in methylated spirits for approximately 2 weeks. Look in a botany book to identify the structures you are observing in your slides.

Roots

A cross-section will reveal what is described in botany

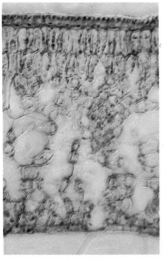

Cross-section of a leaf of a houseplant.

Wood

For cutting methods, compare both drawings on this page; they explain the direction and underlying structure of the different cuts. Wood is a morphologically very interesting plant tissue. It is easy to see the difference between wood from deciduous trees and from conifers. A specialist can even sometimes identify one individual species just by looking at a photomicrograph.

Other Supporting Tissues

When viewing a cross-section

Identifying the different cuts through wood. The annular rings (where narrow and wide lumina touch each other) are parallel to the tangential cut.

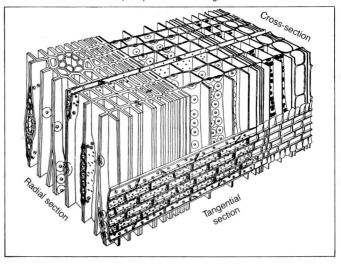

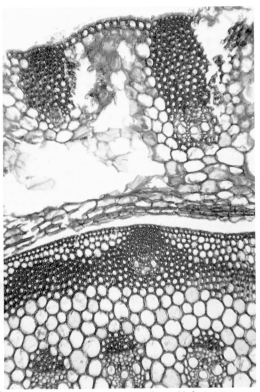

Portion of a cross-section of a stem of a cock's foot grass (*Dactylis glomerata*). The supporting tissues are dyed reddish brown. The top part of the photo shows part of an adjacent leaf; transmitted illumination.

Upper part of photo: Cross-section of a root of a mistletoe (*Viscum album*) growing into soft wood (lower part of the photo). Polarization-interference contrast, combined with oblique illumination.

books. The delicate, small roots of freshly germinated wheat, cleaned and pressed between a slide and a cover glass, are good for examining the cells that turn laterally as they change into root hairs.

Hair and Scales

Stems and leaves are often covered with "hair" and scales, particularly on houseplants. The hair of the stinging nettle is an example; the hairs have easily breakable, glasslike tips.

Filament Hairs of a Stamen

The filament hairs of the *Tradescantia* plant have cells that are a favorite subject for studying the flow of cytoplasm. Use high magnification, high position of the condenser, and oblique illumination.

Onion Skin Membrane

Delicate onion skin is easily obtainable from the inner on-ion layers. If you have a phase-contrast setup, use it here. It will produce good results. Even without staining, with high magnification the nuclei of the cells can be seen, often at different stages of division (see a biology textbook for reference). The different phases of building up a new cell wall in dividing cells are easy to observe. This is consid-ered one of the favorite exer-

87

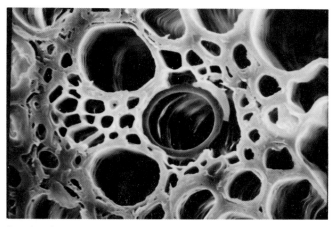

Scanning electron microscopic photo of sections of wood. Above: cross-section. Below: tangential section. The photo below shows clearly the coil-shaped supporting fiber of a large vessel.

of needles; cells of the *Opuntia* and *Oxalis* also contain such inclusions.

Internal Reinforcement
Water-conducting vessels are usually made stiffer by characteristic ringlike or spiral-shaped structures that often look as if they are pulling out, like springs, beyond the edge of the cross-section. The photos to the left are examples taken with a scanning electron microscope.

Starch Granules
Potato starch is the best choice when studying the layered structure of starch granules. Get potato starch directly by scraping a potato. Another choice is some corn starch, like the kind used for starching clothes. Here, the polarization method is best, which you can easily improvise by using two foil disks (or by making use of polarization filters; see photo on page 35).

Pollen
The outer shape of a pollen grain is so differentiated that an expert is often able to determine not only the genus but also the species of plant from just one slide. Pollen from conifers is particularly easy to collect in the spring.

cises for students. You need only one inexpensive and easily purchased stained specimen of onion skin to study the different phases of cell division described in every biology textbook (see the photo on page 89).

Internal Cell Structure
Cells that have bizarre-looking crystal formations inside the cell walls are often found in leaf and stem cross-sections. Calcium oxalate crystals (see photo, page 35) can be found in *Impatiens* as whole bundles

Fruit and Seeds
The development of ovaries into fruit, and also seed development, can be seen in sections through ripening fruit—for example, the fruit on an apple tree. Use low-power magnification and incident il-

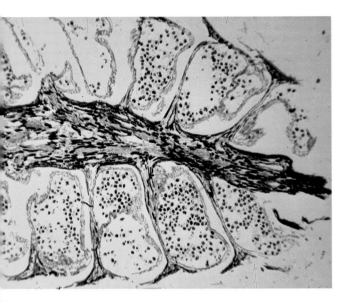

lumination. The structure of a wheat kernel is very interesting. Since it is difficult to get a cross-section from a kernel, you might want to buy a permanent slide. Once you have understood the basic structure, it is easy to follow the changes that take place during the process of germination. Make a cross-section from a fresh wheat sprout. It is best to use incident illumination and low-power magnification.

Vegetative and Bud Meristems

A cross-section of the dark-green node at the end of the branch of an *Elodea* plant shows the budlike structures from which leaves develop. You can observe a similar structure on the growth axil of a shoot of the mare's tail (*Hippuris*), a waterplant.

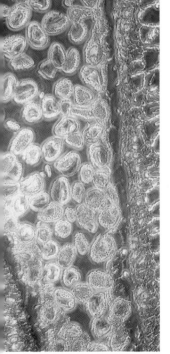

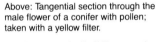

Above: Tangential section through the male flower of a conifer with pollen; taken with a yellow filter.

Left: Filament of a lily (*Lilium* spec.); pollen grains in the center. Positive phase-contrast.

Below: Phases of cell division in onion skin; chromosomes are colored.

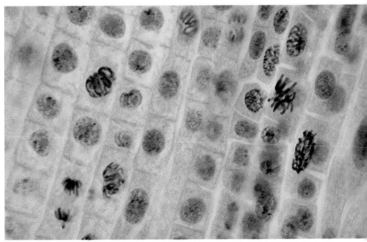

THE ANIMAL KINGDOM

Rewarding choices

Two possibilities come to mind. One can hunt for small animals, like insects or other soil organisms, that fit under the cover glass whole. Or one may specialize in a particular "area of interest," for example, one species, and study its organs. The latter is of no great value to the amateur, who will find out very quickly that specialization requires equipment that is available only to professional laboratories. But for those who are interested, consult the library for information about techniques. I believe that buying permanent slides of whatever you are interested in seems to make more sense and is also much easier than trying to make them yourself.

Every hobby microscopist, however, should go through the process of preparing a small animal, as well as taking samples of tissues for microscopic examination. This is easy to do. I will give you instructions, using the earthworm as an example.

In general, I prefer the "bloodless" method: examining either parts of an animal or whole, small animals. Organisms that live in the water, like small insects, worms, and crustaceans (for instance, isopods), snails and mussels are the easiest to find. Parasites living on other animals are also interesting. Insects' legs, antlers, and chewing parts are easy to prepare, as are their internal organs.

Small Soil Fauna

The easiest way to obtain these small animals is to take some loose sand or earth, as shown in the drawing to the right. The animals are mobilized with a 75-watt light bulb that is suspended about 20 cm (8 in.) above a funnel filled with the medium. The animals will try to escape the heat by moving further and further down into the funnel until they fall into the container underneath. Small soil fauna, e.g., springtails and other very small insects, soil mites, nematodes, insect larvae, beetles, and other small organisms thus may be captured.

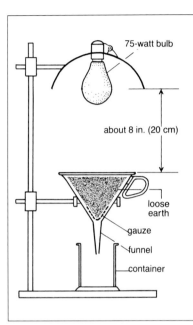

Berlese apparatus used for catching very tiny soil fauna (see text).

Gelatinous spawn of the giant pond snail *Limnaea stagnalis*.

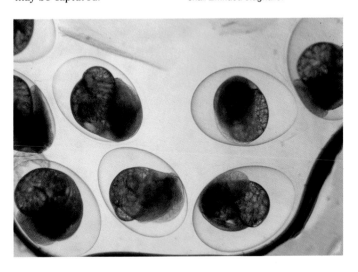

A small fly (Diptera) under low-power magnification. Inside the thorax, the wing and leg muscles can be seen. The specimen was cleared using a special solution.

Animal Development

Observing the spawn of the water snail in various stages of development either in an aquarium or on a stage aquarium is easy to do (see also page 119). Frog eggs can be studied in the same way. However, to obtain and study frog eggs, you may need the permission of the environmental protection agency in your area, as many are endangered species.

In a miniature humidity chamber on the stage, extremely small insects can be preserved and studied for an extended period of time without any problem (see also pages 119 and 122). Some likely choices are: springtails, booklice, bark lice, and small beetles. Under the lowest possible magnification, these animals can be observed while feeding (either on plants or decaying substances), copulating, laying eggs, or moulting.

Preparing an earthworm

In a test tube, immerse an earthworm in 10% alcohol. This will anesthetize and eventually kill the earthworm. The actual dissection is done in a special tray with the bottom coated with a layer of black wax. The tray preparation is described next. Melt beeswax and candle wax together in an empty can over very low heat, on a slightly warm electric stove, not an open flame. When melted, add soot or lampblack to the mixture and

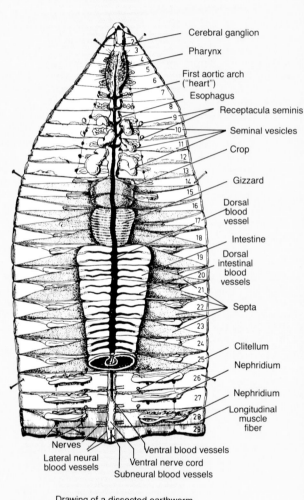

Cerebral ganglion
Pharynx
First aortic arch ("heart")
Esophagus
Receptacula seminis
Seminal vesicles
Crop
Gizzard
Dorsal blood vessel
Intestine
Dorsal intestinal blood vessels
Septa
Clitellum
Nephridium
Nephridium
Longitudinal muscle fiber

Nerves
Lateral neural blood vessels
Ventral blood vessels
Ventral nerve cord
Subneural blood vessels

Drawing of a dissected earthworm. From M. Rehner, *Leitfaden für das Zoologische Praktikum*. Fischer: Stuttgart and New York, 1984.

pour it into the tray. As a dissection tray, a medium-size photographic developing tray is very good.

Then put the earthworm on top of the hardened layer of wax with its dark side facing down. Hold it in place with straight pins at the top and, after slightly pulling the worm straight, at the bottom. The next step is to cut the body open lengthwise from top to bottom with a pointed, very sharp pair of dissection scissors (see page 116) and then unfold the sides so it is open; hold the sides in place with pins.

This procedure lets you view the digestive system (pharynx, esophagus, crop, gizzard, intestines), and the blood vessels running along its length that are attached in looplike fashion to the left and right of the digestive system, specifically around the region of the esophagus and the middle intestines. In the front segments (9 through 13) the paired reproductive organs are found; the size of the seminal vesicles is particularly noteworthy. The septa, very delicate tissue walls, (in the photos slightly distorted during dissection) divide the body into horizontal segments. Inside each segment are elements of the circulatory, digestive, excretory, and nervous systems. If the intestines are cut and lifted out, you can

clearly see the *ventral nerve cord* underneath, the most important part of the nervous system. You will also observe that the intestines show surface-increasing tissue-folds, the *typhlosole*, which are filled with a brownish cell mass, the *chloragogen*. For more a detailed description of the internal structures of the earthworm, consult a zoology textbook.

The Ink Trick
Delicate tissues, like those of the septa and nephridia, are almost white in color and therefore difficult to see under the microscope. But here is a trick to make them come "alive." Cover your specimen with 1 cm of water. Take an old-fashioned indelible blue pencil and hold the tip in the water over the portion you want to mark and wait until

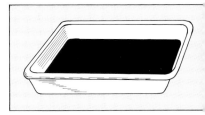

Dissection tray.

some of the dye is dissolved (1 to 3 seconds). The blue coloring (methylene blue) will float into the water and settle on the bottom. All of a sudden your specimen will become three-dimensional. Thousands of details you did not even know existed will take on different shades of blue and be clearly visible. This is a well-tested and at the same time very easy method to make details visible. By varying the length of time that the specimen is exposed to the "ink

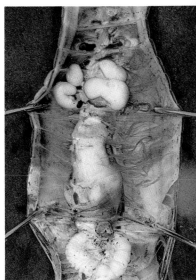

A section of an earthworm specimen, at low magnification. Left: uncolored. Right: stained by the ink trick (see text).

93

pencil," you can control the depth of color. As soon as the proper shade has been achieved (more is not better!) take a pipet and disperse the clouds of color that have settled on top of the specimen.

Microscopic Specimens

Tear off a piece of the stained septum and examine it under a drop of water, covered with a cover glass. Use the same procedure with nephridium tissue; the clitellum is very interesting. The brownish cloragogen give little information. When

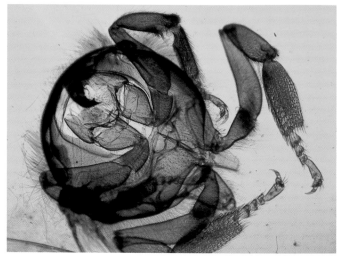

Section of honeybee (*Apis mellifera*), including legs. The chitin was cleared according to the method described on page 99. The large pollen organ of the hind leg (upper right) is heavily covered with hair.

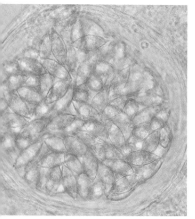

A gregarine (*Monocystis* species) cyst, with boat-shaped sporocysts, is extracted from the seminal vesicles of an earthworm.

examining a piece of the intestine after it has been cleaned, cut open, and spread out, one can observe the intestinal cells on the inside. Use weak magnification and incident illumination. The branching out of neural ganglia is visible when a piece of the ventral

nerve cord is extracted and put under the microscope. The blood vessels that surround the esophagus in looplike fashion have internal aortic loops. Pot-shaped pairs of ovaries are located in the thirteenth section next to the ventral nerve cord. If you use the methylene blue staining method, the eggs in the ovaries will be easily visible; tear out a piece with the smallest pair of tweezers you can find. With a narrow pipet that is broken at an angle at the tip, pierce the seminal vesicle and extract the whitish mass of maturing sperm and transfer it for examination to a microscope slide.

Like other animals, earthworms carry parasites. When examining a sperm suspension, you are guaranteed to

find *gregarines*, parasite protozoa of the *Monocystis* genus, in all stages of development. Next to the long-bodied, large gregarines, the most obvious are *sporocysts*, round, boat-shaped structures that contain eight sporozoites each.

One can often observe tiny little larvae of nematodes located in the loops of the nephridia, like *Rhabditis pellio*, noticeable by their wiggling movements.

Preserving the Earthworm

The rest of the earthworm and other small fauna, as well as tissue samples, can be stored in either 70% alcohol or in 3% to 4% formaldehyde in glass containers that have snap-on tops. Formaldehyde hardens tissues and is therefore partic-

94

ularly useful for future dissection. Think about using methylated spirits instead of the more expensive pure alcohol, and, instead of an expensive container with a snap-on closing, use an empty, transparent film container with an airtight lid. (By the way, such a film container is also an excellent substitute for a micro-aquarium.)

More preparation suggestions

I can recommend the following animals for preparation: garden snails; cockroaches and other large insects (for instance, grasshoppers); small trout (available in fish stores). In the past the green frog was *the* standard animal for microscopic examination; today only zoology students should use them as they are endangered animals. Often the problem of sterilization is raised. No matter what kind of animal you work with, even if you have only dissected small fauna, the tools used should always be sterilized, either by spraying them with disinfectant or by carefully wiping them off with 70% alcohol. Careless handling of dissection instruments can lead to serious infections, particularly when working with laboratory rats or doves.

Easy-to-make specimens

Ink Specimens

One drop of a culture (for instance, of paramecia) is mixed

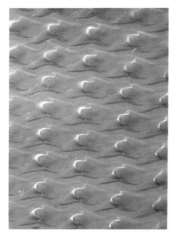

The surface of the radula of an edible snail (*Helix pomatia*). The 3-dimensional effect was achieved by using mixed light and Rheinberg illumination.

Ciliate *Paramecium caudatum*. The opal-blue stain brings out the blue dots of the "cilia pockets," as well as the row of cilia and enclosed crystals at the blue edge.

with an equally large drop of India or drawing ink, then spread out the sample on the glass slide with the edge of the cover glass. After the preparation is dry, you will be able to see the protozoa, which are light on a dark background; under certain circumstances even the cilia and enclosed trichocysts may be visible. The fine ink particles usually settle on the edges and into deeper crevices, highlighting the most delicate structures.

A drop of mounting medium over the specimen and a cover glass are all that is needed to make your specimen permanent. The drop should be large enough so that the medium covers the specimen all the way to the edges of the cover glass when it is put on top.

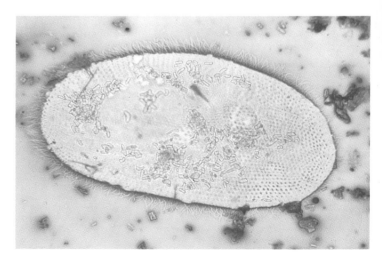

The Smear Method

Ciliates, for example, paramecia can also be prepared by the smear method. One drop containing large numbers of them is mixed with an equally large drop of a 10% opal-blue staining medium, and spread out over the glass slide with the cover glass edge. In about ½ hour, the specimen will be dry and may be covered with

mounting medium. This method allows you to view the tiny "chambers" from which the cilia extend. It is best to view such a specimen with an oil-immersion objective. The photos show how a paramecium looks using several different staining methods and preparations. The procedures are complementary; no single preparation shows everything.

Blood Smears

One of the most famous uses of the smear method is for preparing blood specimens. A drop of animal blood diluted in an isotonic saline solution is spread out on a glass slide with the edge of a cover glass or another slide (see p. 97) and left to dry.

Special staining solutions are used to show the many different types of white blood cells, which you can easily duplicate. First, use a few drops of Jenner's stain (in Europe, called May-Grünwald solution); after 3 minutes add the same number of drops of distilled water. After another min-

ute, the solution is allowed to run off and the preparation is rinsed off with distilled water. Now add Giemsa solution and wait for another 15 minutes. This solution is allowed to run off and the preparation is rinsed with distilled water. The preparation is now allowed to air-dry. Clean the underside of the glass slide, if necessary,

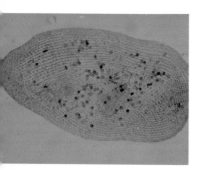

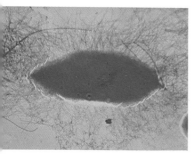

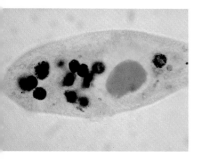

Left: Ciliate *Paramecium caudatum*. Top: Klein's reagent shows silver staining of cilia; green filter. Middle: Dry specimen with extended trichocysts; blue filter. Bottom: Staining of nucleus (red), and food vacuoles, after ingesting ink particles (black).

Right: Blood smears; oil-immersion with 100 × objective. In addition to the anucleate red blood cells, two types of white blood cells are recognizable as well as blood parasites of the genus *Trypanosoma*. Top: 8 × eyepiece, green filter. Bottom: 16 × eyepiece.

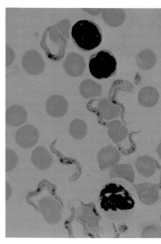

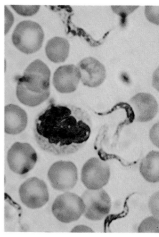

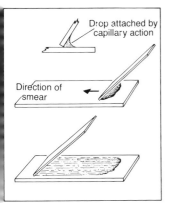

Making a preparation by the smear method.

with 70% alcohol. Cover the preparation with mounting medium. With luck you can now study the red blood cells (pink) and different types of white blood cells (for instance, granulocytes, lymphocytes, and monocytes) that are described in any histology textbook. Viewing is best done with oil-immersion. Of course, such preparations, including those showing blood parasites, can also be purchased.

Preparations by Scraping
With a spatula or the dull side of a knife (after sterilizing it with 70% alcohol or by boiling), gently scrape a sample from the soft tissue from the inside of your cheek. Mix this sample with a drop of water using a dissecting needle, spread the mixture across a glass slide with a cover glass, and cover it with a cover glass. Epithelium cells from the mucosa are particularly easy to

observe using the phase-contrast method. However, the India ink-staining method also brings good results. Briefly hold an ink pencil over your specimen and let a drop of ink dissolve; then either allow the ink to settle, covering the specimen with a cover glass, or allow the liquid to evaporate and then cover with a cover glass. Both methods are very effective for examining sperm cells also.

Preparations by the Tearing Method
Submerge a small sample of a specimen in a drop of water and, using two dissection needles, carefully tear it apart in small pieces. You will always find interesting structures that remained intact during this procedure: individual cells or chains of cells, or other matter in plant specimens, usually crystals; in wood, strengthen-

ing coils in water-carrying vessels; in insects, trachea and other parts.

Preparations by the Pressing Method
Nearly every type of histological specimen can be prepared by pressing it between two glass slides and then examining it under low-power magnification; for instance, muscle tissue, bird feathers, cells from the flesh of a pear, etc.

A feather prepared by the pressing method: pressed between two glass slides with clamps, both then secured with cellophane tape; last, the clamps are removed.

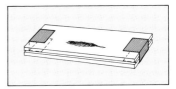

Photo under mixed-light illumination (see page 53), showing small hooks that connect the individual barbs of the feather of a bird in zipperlike fashion.

Dry Preparation Method

Hair, feathers, scales from butterflies and from silverfish (*Lepisma saccharina*), as well as insect wings and other small body parts, can easily be prepared by the dry method. The specimen is simply put on a glass slide, covered with a cover glass, weighted down with a paperweight, and carefully sealed all around with clear lacquer on a fine brush. This will prevent dust from entering and keep the cover glass in place. Dry your specimens beforehand in the oven for about 20 minutes at no more than 120°F (60°C), removing all moisture. Instead of lacquer, you might want to consider using double-sided cellophane tape, as shown in the drawing on this page. This method is suitable only for specimens that are completely dry.

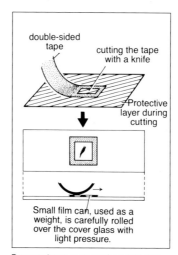

double-sided tape

cutting the tape with a knife

Protective layer during cutting

Small film can, used as a weight, is carefully rolled over the cover glass with light pressure.

Dry specimen, protected against dust, made with the help of a double-sided cellophane tape. Be careful when rolling over the cover glass.

Making Whole-Insect Preparations

Fleas, thrips, or small Hymenoptera can be easily prepared for a permanent collection. Immerse the insect in 70% alcohol, in pure alcohol, and in methyl benzoate for one day each. Attach the insect with a mounting medium. Since a cover glass might squash the insect too much, use thin glass rods as spacers. Specimens that are of uneven height (like insect wings) can be weighted down on the side with a paperweight while the mounting medium is hardening.

Clearing a Specimen

So many parts of insects are worth saving: legs, antennae, chewing apparatus, eyes, poisonous stings, parts of a chitinous shell, even internal organs.

Usually, chitin is very dark, so bleach it for easier viewing, immerse the specimen in chemicals in this order: first, 70% ethyl alcohol; next, 94% alcohol, and then in pure alcohol. Leave it in each one for a few hours. Then put the specimen in methyl benzoate for several days; the longer it is in, the clearer it will become. Instead of methyl benzoate you can also use xylol (do not in-

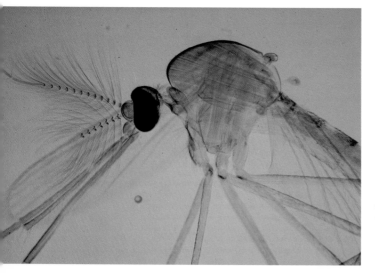

Gnat: whole insect as specimen. Specimen was cleared; then contrast increased with red stain. Flight muscles are visible in the thorax. Plan-objective, no condenser; matte illumination.

Preparation of the proboscis tip of house fly; Rheinberg illumination.

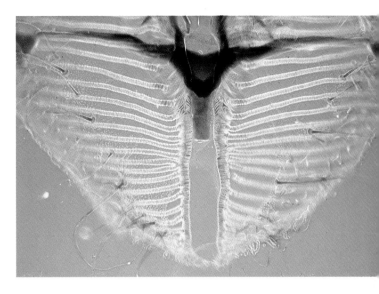

hale it!); but then you must make sure that you wash the specimen carefully in absolute alcohol; close the container, as absolute alcohol absorbs water. As a final touch, you might want to seal the specimen with clear lacquer.

Casting Method

In a small spoon, mix a turpentine substitute with a few drops of household glue and transfer some of the solution to a glass slide. Let it stand until it is almost dry, but still sticky to the touch. Now gently press a butterfly wing onto the surface and then pull it off again. The geometrically arranged scales will stick to the surface. Let it dry overnight, place a cover glass over it, and seal it with a paintbrush in lacquer around the edges.

Macroscopic Specimens

It is not necessary to restrict yourself to microscopic specimens. Sometimes one might just want to save dried miniature insects, seeds, parts of a plant's rind, and many other things. They are very useful for stereomicroscopic viewing or for photomicroscopy with incident illumination and low-power magnification.

In the past I used to stick such parts to a glass slide with a drop of beeswax and store them without a cover. How-

ever, if in the future you want to change the specimen's positioning, you have a bit of work to do. Today I keep these things in clear, empty film canisters with snap-on lids. Later on, they can easily be positioned.

Part of the chewing mandible of a grasshopper.

Permanent Stained Preparations

I do not recommend that you make your own permanent slides, because the process is complicated, takes a long time, and the outcome is seldom what you expected. On the other hand, there is nothing wrong with at least wanting to try it. For that reason I am giving a simple example using an easy specimen stained with haematoxylin– eosin. This double-stain method makes the cell nucleus a dark blue and gives the cytoplasm and other cell structures (like individual muscle fibers) a reddish pink color. The work is done in several stages. Whenever the "cook of the house" decides on pork liver for dinner, ask for a piece the size of 1 cc (⅜ in.^{3}) and start making your specimen as described below.

Fixing

The freshly cut specimen is submerged for a few days in 40% formaldehyde (see page 114).

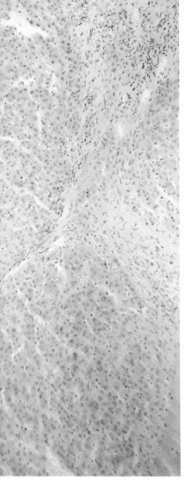

A cross-section of a pork liver lobe, section stained with haematoxylin–eosin solution. The do-it-yourself method, as shown here, seldom produces preparations as good as those made professionally.

Washing

To wash out the chemicals, put the specimen into a cup and allow water from a faucet to drip on it continuously overnight.

Alcohol Bath

Allow the cube to remain in an 70% to 96% alcohol bath for a few days.

Cutting

In a professional laboratory the cube, after all the water has been extracted, is placed in a solution of xylol to remove the alcohol. Next, it would be dipped into liquid wax and then cut into thin slices with a microtome. These sections would then be glued to glass slides. Next, the wax would be washed off with the appropriate solvent and the specimen would be stained.

Since the liver tissue has already hardened sufficiently, we will skip the preliminaries and immediately make our sections, cut as thin as possible, with a razor blade or razor knife, as described on pages 78–79 and 101–102.

Staining

Have a few very small glass containers ready and put a few drops of haematoxylin solution in some and a few drops of eosin solution in others. (Both solutions are available from biological supply houses.) In an additional dish have a few drops of absolute alcohol (or terpineol), and in another dish, a few drops of xylol (xylene). With the tip of a brush, transfer one specimen for 2 minutes first to the haematoxylin dish; then wash out the solution by putting the specimen in water in a coffee cup; then put the same specimen into the dish with the eosin solution for about 2 minutes. Then drain it. The next step is a serious cleansing procedure: begin by first immersing the specimen in 94% alcohol (before that in 70% alcohol if you have it), followed by immersion in absolute alcohol, and lastly in xylol, each for 10 to 20 minutes.

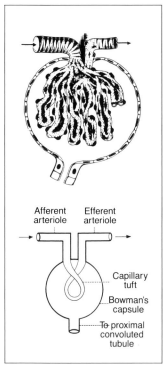

Afferent arteriole

Efferent arteriole

Capillary tuft

Bowman's capsule

To proximal convoluted tubule

Partial schematic drawing of a nephron and its functioning. The urine passes through the tiny branching capillary tuft and is sent out through the proximal convoluted tubule.

Mounting preparations

With the tip of a fine brush, transfer your specimen to a glass slide with a small drop of xylol, stretching it slightly; absorb the excess xylol from the specimen with a paper tissue. Now add a drop of mounting medium and put the cover glass on top, trying not to trap any air between the two glass layers. Let the preparation dry for a few days. *Important note: The mounting medium and xylol are toxic chemicals and should only be used in a well-ventilated area and in small amounts. Avoid inhaling the vapor.*

Examination of the preparation reveals a dark-blue cell nuclei in reddish liver tissue and demarcations typical of pork liver. The fibrous tissue that defines the lobes themselves is not visible; for that to happen, the specimen has to be treated with azan dye. In the center of each lobe is the cavity of the central vein, and in the surrounding tissue are the branched-out capillaries of the portal vein, branches of the liver artery, and the bile duct. The portal vein enters into the lobe and develops into a delicate capillary system.

Of course, you can always use other organs—for instance, a kidney, tongue, or heart—all easily available at the butcher shop. When making a cross-section of a pork kidney, you might be lucky enough to cut through a nephron, as happened in the photo at the right, above. Its basic structure is shown in the drawing on the opposite page.

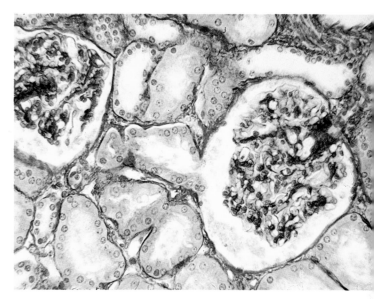

Cross-section of the kidney of a mammal, showing two nephron bodies. On the right side, you can see the cross-section of a blood vessel loop; on the left is the beginning of the efferent tubule; (see the drawing on the opposite page).

Microtome

In general, a hobby microscopist has no need to produce very thin slices of organic matter; if need be, a hand microtome is usually sufficient (see page 78). Microtomes used in laboratories for scientific purposes are heavy and very expensive. There are two different kinds: the sliding microtome, and the rotary microtome. In the first type, the object is stationary and the knife slides along the object's surface. In the latter type, the object is mounted on a gear-driven device and the knife is stationary. After each cut, the object is raised a tiny amount, by about 10 μm. With a bit of experience, one can produce many extremely thin cross-sections from just one cube of

Example of a rotary microtome. This one was made by Microthek.

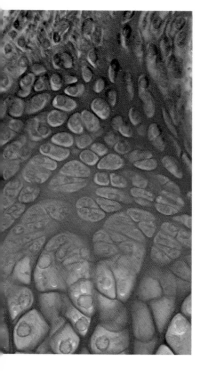

A microtome section of the cartilaginous end of a leg bone of a mouse. Stained, and photographed with polarization–interference contrast.

Spool-microtome. With such an improvisation one cannot expect to produce super-thin sections. It is important that the surface of the washer should not be angled (make sure that it is right side up!).

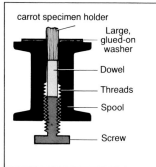

carrot specimen holder

Large, glued-on washer

Dowel

Threads

Spool

Screw

end of an empty spool of thread. Cut screw threads partway through the spool from the other side (see diagram), and insert a dowel piece and a screw that fits the threads. A specimen may easily be wedged between two semicircular holding pieces, which (believe it or not) can be made from a cut carrot. It really works! Turning the screw around moves the specimen toward the blade; experiment with it until you find out how much.

How to use a razor blade, a microtome knife, and a hand microtome has already been discussed on pages 77–79. The hand microtome is the best choice for the microscopist who makes cross-sections only occasionally, but still wants the results to be at least somewhat professional.

organic material, and make a series of sections, from which a three-dimensional histological model can be constructed.

In addition to the above-mentioned expensive microtomes, there are also much smaller, very solid models available that are less expensive. The cost is within reach of amateur microscopists, if tissue sectioning is what they are after. Such microtomes are available from Microthek, Leica, and Edmund Scientific, among others.

However, you can build a passable "microtome" yourself: glue a large, flat washer to one

Cross-section of a human ovary with two follicles.

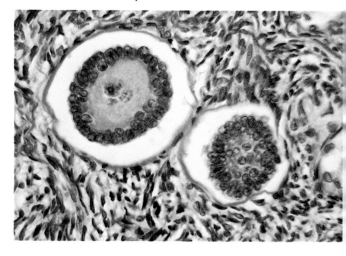

Buying permanent slides

Permanent slides can be bought from biological supply companies. They are also available for a very reasonable price in sets or series. When it comes to human tissue preparations, I always recommend buying ones that have been made by professionals. They usually are double- or triple-stained, and you can choose from samples of heart, muscle, liver, kidney, and—something that is extremely interesting—from organs and vessels that have inner lumens: veins, and small and large intestines. You can also order cross-sections of sense organs from the eye, skin, and ear. Another set of permanent slides that I recommend highly gives information about organ development; for example, the development from cartilage to solid bone, including the calcification process during adolescence. Other examples are cross-sections through the base of a fingernail, in which you can observe the development of a nail; or sections of skin from the scalp, showing hair roots. Such permanent slides ought to be studied with a reliable, well-illustrated textbook at hand. The information that you gather in the process is a reward you will always treasure.

There are many textbooks on histology; some are easily read, even by the lay person. After your study of human histology, you will see yourself in a new light.

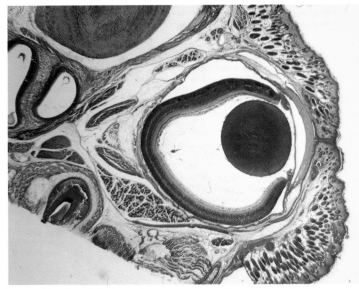

Cross-section through the head of the embryo of a small mammal. On the right, the developing eye; on the left, a tooth bud.

Cross-section through compact bone. Several osteons with central canals and dark-stained bone cells are visible. Goldner's variation of Masson's trichrome stain.

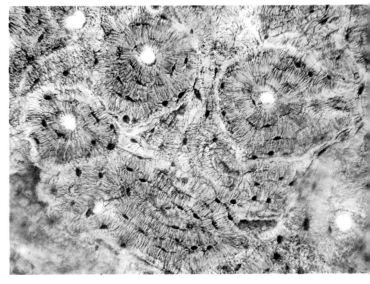

103

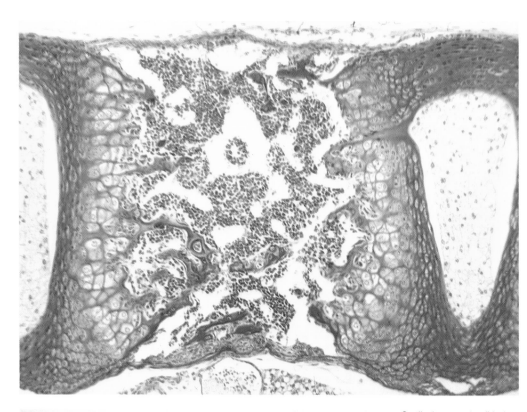

Cartilaginous region (blue) and the beginning stages of bone development (red) in the vertebral column of a mouse.

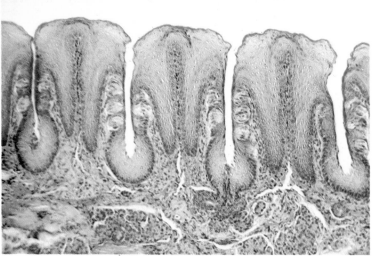

Cross-section of the longitudinal papillae of a rabbit's tongue. On the sides, taste buds are visible. They look like tiny onions. At the bases of the shafts are salivary glands.

Organizing a slide collection

There are several possibilities for storing your slide collection. You could keep them in clear plastic sheets with individual pouches. Slides also can be stored in a booklike slide holder that folds like a map; or they can be organized in a box with individual slots. The maplike arrangement has the advantage of a better overview, which makes reading labels easier. Keeping slides in a slotted box, on the other hand, lets you store more slides in less space. It is best to store the slides horizontally, because liquids in the slides that are not yet completely dry have a tendency to run when slides are stored vertically (see photo on page 79).

The result of most slides of microorganisms, even when the best preparation techniques are used, is usually disappointing. When choosing permanent slides, I would therefore recommend that you concentrate on series of slides that deal with the histology of higher plants, the histology of animals and humans, and embryology. Make sure you know what tissue has been stained with what type of stain and what color it became. That is tremendously helpful when trying to understand the more complex specimens and the histological architecture of the object. The photos on pages 103 and 104 are excellent examples of what good slides should look like.

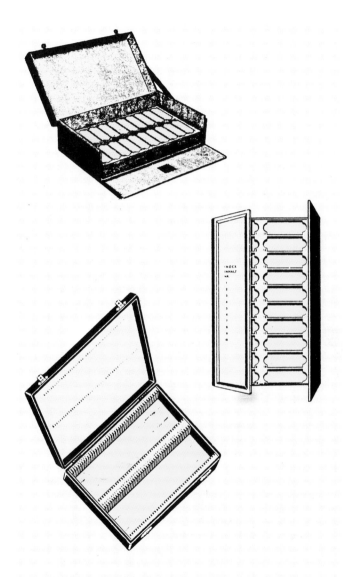

Several possibilities for storing and organizing a slide collection. From top to bottom: a box holding slides in sheets; a folding map-style slide-holder; and a box with slots for 100 slides.

INORGANIC STRUCTURES

Crystallization

One of the favorite "games" of many microscopists is observing the crystallization process, if possible under polarized light. Spread a large drop of water on a glass slide and immerse a crystal in it—for example, simple table salt, or any other kind of salt, or maybe even two or three crystals of different salts. Under low-power magnification, watch how the dissolved salt crystallizes as the water evaporates, sometimes very quickly, often instantly.

The number of different colors created under polarized light is truly amazing, and results in excellent colored photomicrographs. Of the different salts available, it seems that magnesium sulfate or a mixture of sodium chloride and potassium chloride work the best.

Stone sections

Stones can be ground so thin that they become transparent and are suitable for microscopic examination. The process involves repeated grinding with increasingly finer-grit abrasives. As soon as the section is as thin as a leaf,

Crystallized table salt under low-power enlargement with polarizing interference contrast.

Table salt crystals in the process of dissolving, under polarizing interference contrast.

Brightfield photo of a thin rock section.

turn it over and work on the other side. This technique is neither difficult nor complicated, but it is best to observe somebody else doing it before you attempt it. If you are interested, get in touch with the paleontology department of a university and ask for information.

Surface structure

Flat stone chips and stone surfaces lend themselves well to observation under incident illumination or, even better, under oblique illumination. With some experience, you will be able to identify the mineral compounds contained in many stones. For miniature crystals, it is imperative that you have a dissecting stereomicroscope. Don't even try to make photographs with this equipment, however; conventional macrophotography will produce much better results.

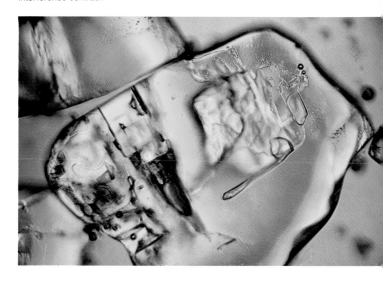

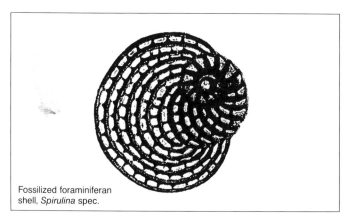

Fossilized foraminiferan shell, *Spirulina* spec.

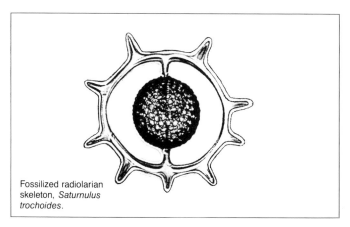

Fossilized radiolarian skeleton, *Saturnulus trochoides*.

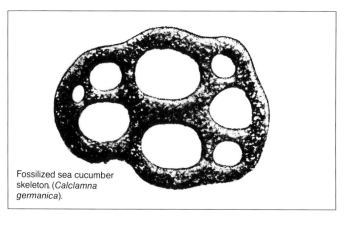

Fossilized sea cucumber skeleton (*Calclamna germanica*).

Microfossils

Tiny microscopic fossils may be found in any mud sample, for instance, in diatomaceous mud; however, these are usually not very old. On the other hand, freshwater or marine diatom deposits often date from the Tertiary Period and the Ice Age. They can be millions of years old and still be remarkably well preserved. In the U.S., large deposits are found in California; there are others in Idaho, Nevada, New York, and Washington. Diatoms are used in the production of dynamite fillers, insulation, and other purposes.

Other microfossils include well-known deposits of calcareous shells of foraminiferans (ocean sand belongs to this category), radiolarians (the most beautiful are in sediments found in Barbados) and silicoflagellates. Others are calcareous flagellates, remnants of exoskeletons of tiny crustaceans, hard parts (sclerites) from the septa of sea cucumbers, sponge spicules, and so forth. All can be harvested by dredging pulverized deposits. Fossils can also be extracted by chemical means; however, that procedure has to be handled with great care. (Consult a book on micropaleontology techniques before proceeding.) If microfossils are embedded in rock, you can also use the abrasion method.

Examining brown coal and peat is also very interesting. Huge amounts of fossilized pollen are found in peat moss.

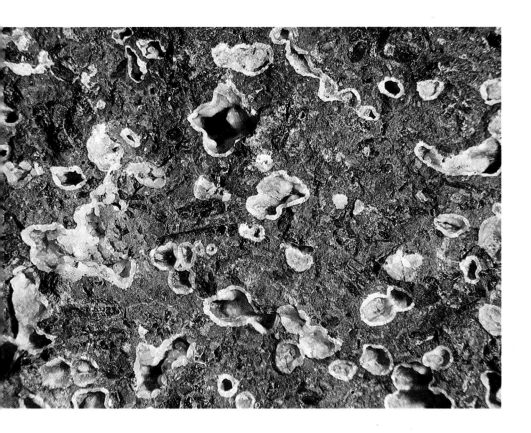

Analyzing pollen allows us to reconstruct rather accurately the climatic changes that occurred from the Ice Age on. Other well-preserved fossils are the shells of shell-bearing amoebas (Arcellinida). See photos on page 137.

Vulcanized rock from the Kaiserstuhl, Germany, taken with incident illumination, a low-power objective (2.5 ×) and a frontlens-diaphragm; image width, about 15 mm.

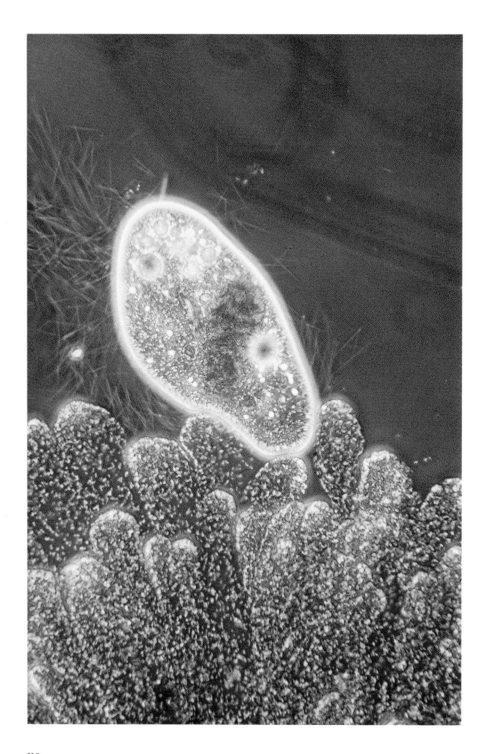

AQUATIC MICROORGANISMS

The hunting ground

What to Look For

Where there is water, there is life. However, a drop of water taken from a large, clear lake would contain live organisms only in the rare circumstances of a heavy "bloom" of micro-organisms. Organisms in open water must be concentrated by plankton nets or by centrifuging before you can easily find them.

To start, I recommend something else. Look for old branches; damp moss on the roof of old buildings; peat moss from marshes; water plants in a meadow; brown, algae-covered stones from the seashore; a rotting leaf in a stream; a scraping from the wall of a drainage ditch—all these are home to fascinating organisms.

You can take whole pieces, like a branch that has broken off a tree or torn-off pieces of algae. Pack them in small containers with snap-on lids (see page 119) or, for much less expensive containers, you can use empty clear-plastic film containers that can be tightly closed. You can also scrape small amounts off a given specimen and store them in a little water in small glass bottles; or you can squeeze the liquid out of moss clumps into a small glass bottle. When you get home, stir the liquid well and then let the contents settle to the bottom. Extract some of what has settled with a pipet, and transfer it to a glass slide.

Where to Look

In general, always switching sampling locations does not yield a greater variety, because different places usually harbor the same organisms. It is much

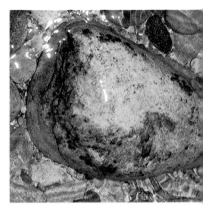

A diatom-covered stone from the shores of Lake Constance, Germany.

better, more productive, and more exciting to visit a few places frequently and follow the development of the organisms that live there over a period of a year. Small ponds and small puddles are ideal, as are slow-moving streams, and rooted or floating plants like reeds, sea lilies, and the like.

Bloom of the blue-green algae *Microcystis aeruginosa* on Lake Federsee. These algae, when present in large amounts, are responsible for the green color of water; the algae's waste products make swimming in such places dangerous.

Ciliate with released trichocysts next to an outgrowth of bacteria (*Zoogloea ramigera*); phase contrast; somewhat flattened out.

Small ponds in particular are home to an astounding variety of organisms, which vary throughout the year. Early in the spring, water blooms of free-floating organisms begin to grow a great deal. Sometimes the pond seems to be filled with enchanting green algae; the next thing you know, tiny rotifers have taken over, only to be replaced by masses of tiny ciliates. A microscopist can be kept busy all year—often several years—by a small pond, without ever becoming bored.

The samples you have taken home need to be checked regularly. As with a hay infusion (see page 120), the population often changes dramatically over time. A jar on a windowsill filled with water from the pond, with perhaps living plants and some sediment on the bottom, protected against strong sunlight, becomes a miniature pond that allows you to make new discoveries all year long.

Collecting

Containers for Transport

Jars. Small preserves jars with screw-on covers and a watertight gasket inside the cover are excellent for taking larger water samples, and they cost you practically nothing. If you take home several samples from a pond, these jars might become a bit unwieldy, however.

Test Tubes. I prefer to use test tubes, available from chemistry supply stores. They come in several different sizes, with either screw-on or snap-on tops. Those that are 1¼ in. (3 cm) wide and 3 in. (7 cm) long are very practical. They can be labeled with an indelible pen (the writing comes off with 70% alcohol) and can be kept as "miniature aquariums" (raise the tops slightly) on a cool windowsill for weeks and even months, always ready to be examined.

Tools for Catching Specimens

All-Purpose Pocket Knife. Pocket knives that come with whole series of accessories are very handy. Look for one with a small saw for cutting twigs that have fallen into the water and a blade for

A plankton net; the collecting chamber is held by a bayonet locking mechanism.

splitting wooden specimens or lifting off moss pads. If possible, it should have a small magnifying glass, a pair of scissors for cutting plant specimens, and a chisel to pry loose hard specimens.

Soup Ladle. An old aluminum ladle, if possible with a sharp edge, is very practical for scraping off sessile organisms. A small discarded kitchen ladle serves well when collecting water from small puddles.

Fishing Net. Fishing nets are also very practical for removing plants from the water and for scraping along the bottom of a pond or puddle. They are available in garden hobby shops and can be tied to a stick, fishing rod, or metal pole.

Sieve. A small strainer from the kitchen, for example a coffee strainer, with a plastic rim and fine nylon netting is very good for collecting tiny worms or insect larvae and the like. Look for it in a gourmet shop or kitchen supply store.

A large, bowl-shaped strainer, about 8 in. (20 cm) wide, with strong, galvanized wire mesh, can be tied to a broomstick to make an ideal and inexpensive instrument for fishing small animals out from among the many plants present in a pond.

Plankton net. If you want to study organisms that live in open water, you won't be able to do without a plankton net. Try to avoid buying one with an extremely dense mesh, because it tends to clog up easily and won't let a sufficient amount of water flow through. Medium-sized mesh (#18, 77 to 86 μm, or about .003 to .0035 in.) is much better, and you can still catch enough small organisms, even the larger ciliates.

Plankton nets also often are sold with a collection tube, but if necessary, you can easily make one yourself from a tall can. Such a tube is practical when you use the net at the bottom of a peat bog or a small pond, because the net can become tangled and torn easily, particularly if part of the "catch" is trash, carelessly discarded by people.

An old-fashioned hand centrifuge from Kosmos.

handle turned the centrifuge for about 2 minutes causing the sediment to collect at the bottom of the test tube; the remaining liquid was discarded. The last drops remaining in the tube are carefully extracted with a pipet and transferred to a glass slide for observation. This procedure is very practical, for I can concentrate all the organisms that were in an egg-cup full of water into a drop of water. Although electric-powered laboratory microcentrifuges are expensive, some personal microcentrifuges are less expensive, like the one from Carolina Biological Supply Company.

White bowl
A round or oblong white plastic dish, about 8 in. (20 cm) wide, is extremely useful for presorting your water samples. As the contents of a ladle or net contrast with the white

Preparing your catch

The specimens you collect must be sorted out as well as prepared. It is always good to do the initial sorting at the site in the field. Sparse plankton specimens can be separated at home with the help of a centrifuge.

Microcentrifuge
In the early days, people used a hand-centrifuge: a crank

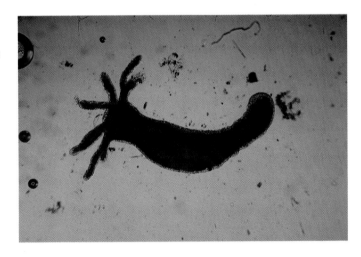

With a white bowl as the container, hard-to-see organisms are easier to find in your catch. Here you can even observe a freshwater polyp (about 6 mm long), in the process of stretching its tentacles.

background, you can easily see organisms as small as .01 in. (¼ mm) with the naked eye.

As is obvious, very little is needed to hunt those tiny organisms. Best of all, everything is very inexpensive. You can make most of the equipment yourself, and the rest are items you can find easily. A trip to a cosmetics or kitchen supply department of a department store will pay off handsomely in useful items.

Fixing and preparation

Examining microfauna and flora is best done when they are fresh. Otherwise, they must be fixed, which means that they have to be preserved against organic decomposition and undergo specific preparation, such as staining (see page 100).

Fixing Solutions

Alcohol. In most cases, 70% alcohol is very useful; however, I do not recommend examining specimens that have been treated with a fixing solution. If you have something particularly interesting, use the fixative method only for making reference slides, and do this only *after* you have examined your unfixed specimens.
Formaldehyde. Use a 3% solution of formaldehyde, made by diluting a 40% solution as follows: 1 part formaldehyde to approximately 13 parts of water. 40% formaldehyde is available in stores dealing with chemistry and microscopy ac-

cessories. Formaldehyde has a very unpleasant odor and is detrimental to your health, so work in a very well-ventilated place.

Examination Containers
Petri Dishes. These are flat, round glass dishes, available in chemistry and microscopy accessory shops and catalogs. Use a petri dish to transfer a thin layer—about .2 in. (½ cm)—of a given sample for examination with a stereo inspection microscope (p. 115, left).
Watch Glasses. These glass dishes are slightly curved and about 1¼ in. to 2½ in. wide (3 to 6 cm). They are excellent for collecting water when there is only a small amount available to begin with, because whatever is in this dish automatically collects at the deepest point.

Square Watch Glasses.
These small, square, heavy glass blocks have a hollow in the center. They are practical; because of their considerable weight, they can't easily be moved about. They also are used when there is only a small amount of water available.

Using a stereomicroscope

For surveying water samples at home in a petri dish, a watch glass, etc., I strongly recommend that you use a stereo inspection microscope. Magnification of between 8× and 12× is perfectly sufficient. Less-well-known manufacturers have constructed instruments that are quite acceptable. They are really very good and not very expensive.

Square watch glasses, about 1¼ in. (3 cm) across.

Right: improvised incident and transmitted light using two small lamps, added to an old stereomicroscope, is ideal for surveying samples.

Left: A stereo inspection microscope that is well suited for examining plankton; it comes equipped with a supplementary magnifying lens and has a good working distance (Wild MIO from Leica).

Illumination

You can look at your samples through a stereomicroscope with reflected, transmitted, or mixed illumination. Take an angled block of wood and glue a glass plate on top as a protruding stage, put a pocket mirror obliquely under it, adding two lamps for transmitted and reflected illumination. Miniature lamps with swing-out arms, like those used for reading in bed, are ideal; use round light bulbs between 25 and 40 W. Better yet are lamps with a telescopic arm, 6 V and 15 to 25 W (like the lamps in car roofs). Many different types of desk lamps are also available that have low-voltage bulbs and already come with a stand. Make sure that the arm can be easily and securely raised and moved out of the way.

Black-and-White Plate

A glass plate, about 6 in. × 6 in. (15 cm × 15 cm), with black paper glued to half of the underside and white paper to the other half, is very useful. A white kitchen tile with one half covered with black paper also works well. Using it, you can instantly change from a dark to bright background. For surveying some organisms, a bright background is better; for others, a dark background is preferable. But don't hesitate to experiment. Make sure that you devise a quick and easy way of switching from black to white background.

Working with minute amounts of water

Working with very little water is standard when making mi-

croscopic preparations; transferring small amounts from a dish to a glass slide is always done with a pipet.

Pipet

Pipets are glass tubes on which one end is more or less elongated and the other end is equipped with a rubber bulb. They are available in shops that carry accessories for chemistry work. Applying varying amounts of pressure to the bulb allows you to extract as much or as little water (containing the tiny organisms) as you want. Releasing the pressure on the bulb lets the water flow out, onto either a glass slide or a watch glass, for example.

Extracting Larger Organisms

A water flea, only 1/16″ long (1.5 mm), is considered a giant

115

in the microscopic universe. The best way to catch it is with a pipet that is open on the top (no cap attached) and has a relatively wide opening on the end. Immerse the pipet in the water and wait until the crustacean is inside. Close the top by putting your thumb over it, and lift the glass tube out of the water. Hold the pipet vertically over a glass microslide, remove your thumb, and let the water plus the organism flow out. Of course, a normal pipet with a rubber cap can also be used, as long as the catching end is at least 3 mm in inner diameter.

Tools for Dissection

Not all the tools listed here are necessary for examining the world in a drop of water, but some are important for the dissection of plant and animal specimens.

Forceps. These can be bought either in a microscopy specialty store or in a watchmaker's shop. Tweezers that you find in a cosmetics kit won't do, because they are too short and clumsy. Forceps should have long handles, be well-balanced and, most of all, should have fine points that close securely when squeezed together.

Dissection Needle. You can buy dissection needles, but you can also make them yourself by inserting either a thin or thick sewing needle into a wooden handle.

Dissection Needle with Cutting Edges. This needle has been slightly flattened at the end, creating two cutting edges. Dissection needles are ideal for removing and tearing off portions of insects or small crustaceans.

Spear-point Needles. The spear-shaped needles that are available in specialty shops are very elegant. They are ideal for transferring flat plant spec-

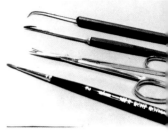

Curved dissection needle, spear-point needle, a pair of dissection scissors, and a brush made from the very soft marten hair.

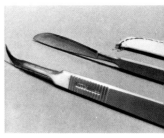

One-piece scalpel with protective cover and scalpel with a clamp-in disposable blade.

imens from one solution to another; they are also very handy for moving, stirring, and dividing objects under the stereo inspection microscope, as well as for separating parts of an animal's body.

Scalpel. For dissections of small animals, in general, a scalpel is an absolute necessity. The hobby microscopist, on the other hand, could probably manage without it.

Disposable Razor Knives. These consist of sharp blades that can be inserted in a metal handle, and replaced when they get dull. Break-off hobby or craft knives are also made. Both provide

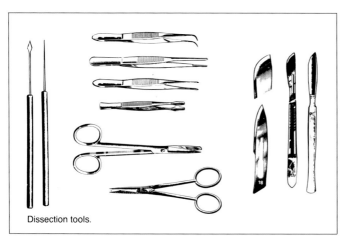

Dissection tools.

you with a sharp blade every time you need it.

Brush. Delicate, very pointed brushes made from animal hair are not only treasured by painters. Microscopists use these brushes to transfer delicate microorganisms.

Syringe. Disposable syringes are inexpensive and are ideal for transferring tiny drops of dissolving solutions, filling small dishes with water, or transferring a water drop to a glass slide.

Scissors. A pair of scissors for dissection use should have a fine point and be of good quality. Scissors from your nail kit won't do; good ones are designed specifically for your purpose, and you can be sure they are not inexpensive.

weeks and months. I am not talking about the "modern" aquarium that is used to give a home to fish and water plants. I mean the simple glass container that substitutes for a pond. It includes a solid layer of mud on the bottom, many different plants, and stones. Pumps and filter are never necessary. Such an enclosed pond is the perfect environment for insect larvae, *Tubifex* worms, small water snails that lay their eggs on the wall of the glass, isopods, freshwater polyps, and whatever else has made its home in the stagnant water.

The microscopist can use

several tools to take specimens out of the tank, either a long pipet that goes all the way down into the mud, or a lancet blade which scrapes a layer of tissue off a plant. Algae fibers, gently shredded on a glass slide, often reveal a rich protozoan environment. Water insects often have a film of ciliates on the surface of their bodies. Most of the live organisms, however, are found on the glass itself, particularly in the few millimeters just at the contact zone with the air, where most microscopic life flourishes. The advantage: any growth taking place within the surface build-up can be ob-

Where to keep your "treasures"

The aquarium

An aquarium is not called "a world in a glass" by accident. Every aquarium owner knows that this world changes all the time, sometimes in a matter of

A richly populated pond aquarium, here with a giant pond snail (*Limnaea stagnalis*) and duckweed (*Lemna trisulca*), offers many layers of microorganisms. In addition to the animals and plants themselves, very interesting organisms can be found on the wall of the glass container, particularly in the contact zone where air and water meet. Do not forget to take samples from the muddy bottom also.

A miniature aquarium with scaffolding that allows for the shifting and focusing of an aquarium microscope. I have never owned an aquarium larger than this; a 3-gallon (twelve-liter) tank is enough for this purpose.

aquarium (it is only turned on during observation), or you can use a point light source that illuminates the glass wall from above.

One can also make photos through an aquarium microscope. With a bit of ingenuity and manual dexterity, you can add a camera to your aquarium microscope.

Where to keep specimens

Jelly-Jar Cultures

A workable and at the same time inexpensive way of keeping a culture of microorganisms is to fill an empty jelly jar with some of the water in which you found your specimen. Supply oxygen by adding water-thyme (*Elodea canadensis*) to the jar. With a nail, punch a few holes (even one is sufficient) in the lid, close the jar, and place it in a bright location that is not too warm (northern exposure is best). A jelly-jar culture can be kept for years, provided that the water has nutrients and that, every now and then, you find the organisms are reproducing well. So get busy and make yourself your very own miniature aquarium.

Of course, you could also buy more sophisticated round

served very easily with a strong magnifying glass, and anything interesting can be removed with a single-edged razor blade. A spear-point needle, held at an angle, is very good for transferring small specimens in a drop of water onto a glass slide without disturbing them.

Aquarium Microscope

If you by any chance have an old microscope and can dismantle it, you have almost all you need to build yourself a fine aquarium microscope. A microscope consisting of objective, tube, and eyepiece is mounted in such a way that the optical axis is perpendicu-

lar to the side of the glass aquarium wall. I recommend that you use low-power magnification (10× objective and, at the most, 10× eyepiece). Focus the microscope on an interesting spot and visit that site several times; it is an ideal way to observe the different developmental stages of growth without disturbing the whole population. Snail eggs can be observed in that way, and their development can be followed. I can highly recommend creating such a structure to all who are handy (see photo).

For illumination, you can either place a frosted light bulb on the opposite side of the

glass containers with snap-on lids. Those that I buy have an airtight lid and are 3½ inches (9 cm) tall and 2 inches (5 cm) wide. It is important to either leave the airtight lids slightly ajar, or to punch one or two small holes in the lid. I always have at least two or three dozen "micro-aquariums" growing at any one time. Lately, I have switched over to film-canister "mini-aquariums," made out of empty, clear plastic 35-mm film canisters; the microorganisms seem to be doing just as well in the mini-aquariums.

Microscope-Slide Aquarium
In addition to the aquariums we have discussed so far, let's take a look at a mini-microaquarium: one made of a single drop of water on a slide.

Old cultures in 2-inch (5-cm) glass containers.

This drop also contains a "balanced" and alive miniature environment, and it can be kept balanced if you prevent the water from evaporating.

You can take a normal spec-

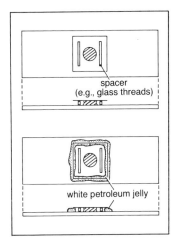
Mini-microaquarium on a slide. Top: exposed to air. Bottom: sealed.

imen that is not too thick, make oxygen available by adding oxygen-producing *Chlorella* algae, and surround the drop of water with a thick layer of petroleum jelly to prevent evaporation. In order to keep the water layer thin enough, we recommend that you use either the wax method (discussed in more detail on page 122), or one in which you put thin glass threads between the microscope slide and the cover glass. Preparations treated in such a fashion are useful for several days, provided they have not been kept too warm.

Cover-Glass Cultures
Transfer a tiny drop that contains the organisms you want to observe to a cover glass, including, if need be, *Chlorella* algae. Turn the cover glass

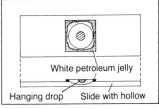
Hanging drop on a concavity slide.

over and place it on a glass microscope slide with a hollow (a concavity slide). Be sure to have put a ring of petroleum jelly around the hollow. Press down gently on the cover glass to make the preparation airtight. If the drop of water is small enough, it will hang on the underside of the cover glass, never touching the glass slide; this is called a hanging drop. This is a wonderful way of observing cell division and the different developmental stages of bacteria and the like.

Culturing microorganisms

Using Water from the Source
The difference between keeping and culturing microorganisms is, in practical terms, purely academic. If water contains a sufficient amount of nutrients, microorganisms will grow and multiply very well, often even better than you may have expected. Clever mi-

119

croscopists will start their cultures by using water from the source where the specimens were found, putting it in containers that are not too small, and adding only a small amount of the relevant material to it—for example, mud, pieces of twigs, or leaf remnants. The best containers for such cultures are the "film-canister aquariums."

Hay Infusion
This is a classic technique and still one of the best. Put a suitable substrate in a jelly jar, fill it with regular, long-standing tap water, and add a little water from the pond to it, or pond sediment. One possible substrate is hay—not too much; a small handful to each quart (liter) of water. Salad leaves (it does not matter if they have started to decompose), or dried kohlrabi slices are also good choices.

In as little as one to two days, you will notice a film forming on the surface of the water that contains microorganisms, mostly ciliates, which feed on the hay microbes. Sometimes a big white cloud of paramecia forms further down around the substrate. Certain species of microorganisms appear, developing and reproducing, until they reach a certain number; then they disappear again, making room for another group. Since constant change is taking place within the environment of the hay infusion, you will never be bored when you remove a small portion of the surface layer for observation.

Soil Infusion
Take a 1-quart (1 liter) glass container, cover the bottom with a ⅜-inch-thick (1-cm) layer of garden soil, and add 8 oz. (½ liter) of standing tap water. Transfer the mixture to an old, discarded stainless steel pot, and boil for ½ hour. Add an inoculation of algae (for instance, scraped off a leaf, or a small inoculation of filamentous algae) to the liquid. They will survive well in such a soil culture, when placed in a Mason jar whose cover has had the rubber gasket removed prior to closing it.

Milk Cultures
An empty preserves jar, half-

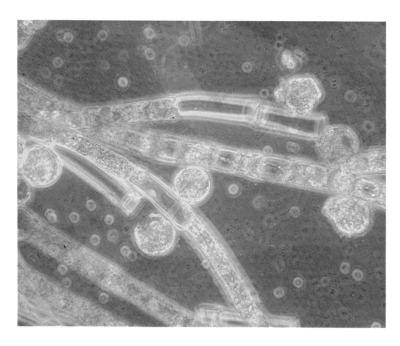

Green algae, *Oedogonium cardiacum*, with motile spore that have already separated. The reproductive bodies usually develop when the quality of the environment is diminished. This specimen was kept for 48 hours in a "microscope-slide aquarium" (see page 119). Phase-contrast photography.

way filled with a waste water infusion, harbors many ciliates that eat bacteria. Add one to three drops of milk to the liquid, stir it well, and let it stand. Add another one to three drops after the liquid has become completely clear. This is an ideal environment for huge numbers of paramecia or *Stentor* to develop.

Commercial Nutrient Media

Several microbiological nutritional media are commercially available for growing pure cultures of various organisms. More information on how to make them yourself can be found in more specialized literature.

The hobby microscopist usually has little use for commercially prepared media, because they require special attention and time-consuming care. I would recommend instead using a number of parallel homemade nutrient media solutions in small glasses. Those that do not grow or that start to decay are simply thrown out. Enough will remain that will keep well without any special effort or care on your part. I believe this is the better method.

Live specimens

Microscope Slide

The dimensions of a standard glass microscope slide is 3 inches × 1 inch (76 mm × 26 mm); its thickness is about .04 inch (1 mm). They have either cut or smooth edges and come 50 to a box. The smooth-edged ones are about 50% more expensive than those with simple cut edges, but the danger of cutting yourself is eliminated. Glass concavity slides have the same length and width; however, they are about .08 inch (2 mm) thicker. They have an indented center. I recommend them for hanging drop cultures (see page 119).

Cover Glass

I recommend using cover glasses of thickness 0.15 to .16 mm (see page 33). They are either square or round, or rectangular. I recommend square cover glasses, 18 mm × 18 mm, for general use. Other sizes are 12 mm × 12 mm, 15 mm × 15 mm, 20 mm × 20 mm, 22 mm × 22 mm, and 25 mm × 25 mm, as well as rectangular cover glasses (24 mm × 40 mm) for larger specimens.

Putting a Drop of Water on a Slide

Hold a pipet with a narrow tip carefully over a glass slide. Applying gentle pressure to the rubber bulb, allow a drop of water to fall on the surface of the glass slide. The drop is of the ideal size when the cover glass is completely filled to the edges with water, but does not start to swim around (as it will if the drop is too large). If the cover glass pulls in air and squashes the thicker objects, the water drop is too small. In other words, the size of the drop has to be *just right*.

Placing the Cover Glass

Never let the cover glass just

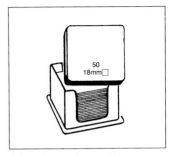

A box of cover glasses with indentation for easy removal.

fall down over the drop of water. Rather, set one side of the cover glass on the microscope slide, propped up on a dissection needle or the nail of your left hand's forefinger. Keep the opposite side of the cover glass raised at an angle. Using either the thumb and forefinger of

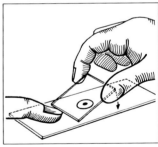

Placing the cover glass using fingers (top) and with two dissection needles (bottom).

your right hand or a second dissection needle, adjust the cover glass so it will be centered over the drop. Then either pull the second needle away or remove your fingernail, and let the cover glass down gently from a small height (³⁄₁₆ inch or 5 mm). See drawings.

Controlling the Thickness of the Water Layer

If the layer of water is too thin between the microscope slide and the cover glass, air bubbles will form underneath the cover glass and distort the image of the object. The answer is a pipet with an extremely

The drop of water from the pipet will be sucked under the cover glass.

small opening at the end, with which a small drop of water can be added when it is positioned at an angle at the side of the cover glass. Capillary action will pull the drop under the cover glass. If the layer of water is too thick, hold a piece of filter paper (coffee filter) or a piece of paper tissue at an angle and allow the excess water to be absorbed. One may, of course, also combine both methods by adding water on one side with the pipet and let-

ting it be absorbed on the other side with a tissue. This is also a way to proceed when you want to stain an already covered specimen.

Special Cases: Thick Water Layers

To observe larger objects under low-power magnification, it may be necessary to have a more substantial layer of water (up to 1 or 2 mm thick). One way of getting it uses glass threads as spacers. To make them, hold the middle of a long glass rod or tube over a gas jet and pull gently on both ends; the degree of pulling will determine the thickness of the thread. Make a few threads of different thicknesses. Break them into small pieces, and put two on opposite sides of the drop of water you want to study on a slide (see drawing on page 119). Then put the cover glass on top of them. In this instance, you need a larger drop of water; of course, you can always add water by the capillary method, if necessary. Pieces of matches, splintered lengthwise with a razor blade, can be used instead of glass threads.

Cover glass "feet". For working with a "thick" layer of wa-

Creating cover-glass "feet" of wax.

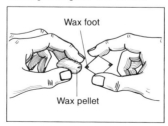

Wax foot

Wax pellet

ter, we can raise the height of the cover glass on wax feet, prepared as follows. In an old can over a double-boiler of hot water, melt a small amount of equal parts of candle wax and beeswax, mix them together, and let cool. (Some people recommend 2 parts of beeswax and 1 part of Venetian turpentine). Shape the wax into little pellets, about the size of a cherry pit. Make four cover-glass feet by brushing each corner of the cover glass over the pellet (all on the same side of the glass, of course). If the wax gets too hard, just knead it for 15 seconds between thumb and forefinger to soften it.

The advantage of this method is that you can vary the distance between the microscope slide and cover glass by varying the pressure with which you push down the cover slip at the corners (use a pencil stump or fingernail). This works well, for example, when a lively waterflea or rotifer has to be lightly compressed and restrained.

Even small organisms like worms can be made to stay put by gently pressing on the cover glass, flattening the specimen out a bit and thereby assuring that it is more in the focal plane. The only disadvantage is that with this method, the movement of the organisms is reduced. But it works well with organs and organelles.

Catching a Specimen
The best way of getting a specimen onto a glass slide is to

extract it, water and all, with a pipet, and then transfer it to a glass slide. To add a specimen to a drop of water already on the glass slide is much more difficult. If, however, you want to do it anyhow, it is best to use a slightly sharpened dissection needle. It is possible to lift a small waterflea or some algae out of a petri dish by holding the needle at an angle. A brush with a very fine point also works well.

Preventing Dehydration

If you want to observe a specimen for a long period of time, you might first want to put a ring of petroleum jelly on the glass slide, put a drop of water containing the organism inside the ring, and put the cover glass on top of it. Slight pressure applied to the cover glass will seal the object safely in its environment. You can also make a circle out of a thick wool fiber, wound in a circle, that has been saturated with water. Proceed as above and protect the specimen with a cover glass. This truly famous and simple trick has another advantage: if you suck out water through the circle, the specimen cannot be sucked out with it. In addition, you could add a small drop of water on the left and right of the fiber with a pipet, until the cover glass is swimming on top of the water, and you could cover it with an inverted petri dish to prevent evaporation.

A miniature "humidity chamber" can be constructed in the following way: with a small hammer, smash an old

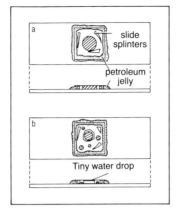

Miniature "humidity chamber." Above: thick. Below: thin.

glass slide. Be sure to wear safety glasses. Suitable oblong pieces create space for a humidity chamber as thick as the glass slide you broke (see drawing a). If you put a somewhat round piece in the middle you have created a microchamber for a tiny little drop (see drawing b). In this instance, in order to keep the content moist, add a few tiny drops within the chamber itself with a pipet. In any case, use petroleum jelly to make the chamber airtight.

Choosing microorganisms

Even though the magic world inside a drop of water is truly amazing, we know there can be too much of a good thing. For example, in my region of the world alone, we have several thousand species of microscopic animals and plants—some that are very rare, and many that are present in abundance. How do you find your favorite in the face of plenty? This is often very discouraging for the beginner. Two methods are available: both are very helpful. One is to try to familiarize yourself personally, so to speak, with the microorganisms that are available in greater numbers. Observing a pond aquarium for a whole year, perhaps, will have taught you how to distinguish among a hundred different microorganisms, and you will be able to identify those that exist in sufficiently large numbers.

On the other hand, one might want to take a theoretical approach by trying to learn the characteristics of each different taxonomic division of living organisms: family, class, order, genus, species. However, this requires an intense study over several years; in the end one usually must narrow the choice down to what seems to hold the most interest, because it is an almost impossible task trying to gain a complete overview of the whole.

I like to recommend proceeding on two parallel tracks: make a list of the most common genera in your area and draw them; then try to learn about the most important characteristics of their members. It should be possible in a relatively short time to identify a typical amoeba, ciliate, *Turbellaria*, or rotifer, crustacean, or small insect. In the case of algae, you will be able to distinguish among the various kinds. The following pages show some typical shapes.

Examples of typical

Here and on the opposite page are

1. Unbranched nonfilamentous bacteria (Eubacteriales)

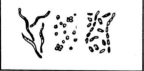

2. Filamentous bacteria (Chlamydobacteriales)

3. Thick blue-green algae (Cyanobacteria)

7. Bilaterally symmetric diatoms (Bacillariophyceae)

8. Yellow-green algae (Xanthophyceae)

9. Euglenoids (Euglenida)

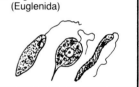

13. Flat nonflagellate unicellular green algae (Chlorococcales)

14. Compact nonflagellate unicellular green algae (Chlorococcales)

15. Filamentous unbranched green algae (Ulotrichales)

19. Filamentous "pond scum" green algae (Zygnemataceae)

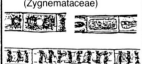

20. Saccoderm desmids (Mesotaeniaceae)

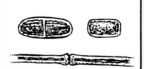

21. Desmids (Desmidiaceae)

freshwater microflora

simple drawings giving an initial overview.*

4. Filamentous blue-green algae (Cyanobacteria)

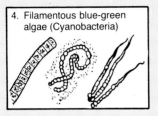

5. Golden algae (Chrysophyceae)

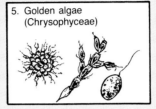

6. Radially symmetric diatoms (Bacillariophyceae)

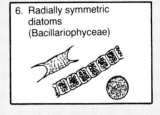

10. Dinoflagellates (Pyrrophyta)

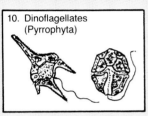

11. Cryptomonads (Phytomastigophorea)

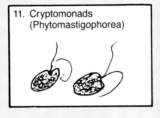

12. Flagellate unicellular and colonial green algae (Volvocales)

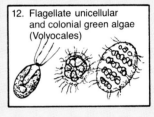

16. Filamentous branched green algae (Chaetophorales)

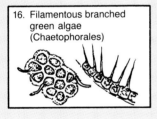

17. Filamentous green algae with distinct egg and sperm (Oedogoniales)

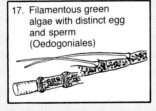

18. Branching filamentous multinucleate green algae (Cladophorales)

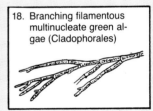

22. Red algae (Rhodophyta)

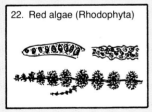

23. Brown algae (Phaeophyta)

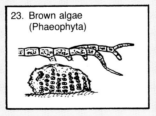

24. Fungi

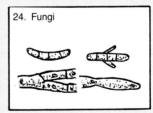

*Be aware that classifications change as knowledge evolves.

Examples of typical freshwater

This page and the following one have simple drawings that give an initial

1. Zooflagellates (Zoomastigophorea) 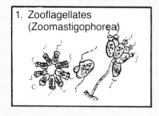	2. Naked amoeba (Amoebida) 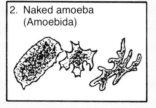	3. Amoeba with shells (Arcellinida) 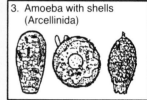
7. Crowned ciliates (Peritrichia) 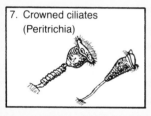	8. Spirotrichea 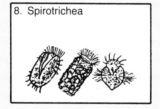	9. Suctoria 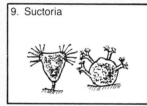
13. Leech-shaped rotifers (Rotifera) 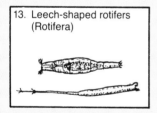	14. Free-swimming rotifers (Rotifera) 	15. Sessile rotifers (Rotifera) 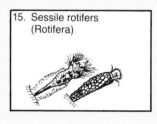
19. Water fleas (Phyllopoda) 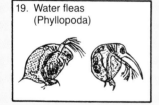	20. Copepods (Copepoda) 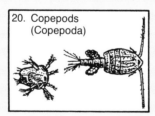	21. Seed shrimp (Ostracoda) 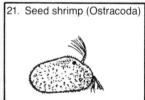

microfauna (not including insects)

overview of the most common freshwater microfauna.

4. Heliozoans (Heliozoa)

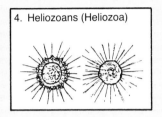

5. Long ciliates (Litostomatea)

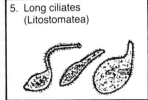

6. Compact ciliates (Nassophorea)

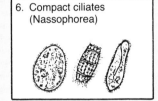

10. Sponges (Porifera)

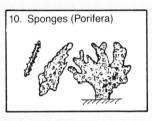

11. Coelenterates (Cnidaria)

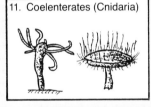

12. Flatworms (Turbellaria)

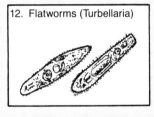

16. Gastrotrichs (Gastrotricha)

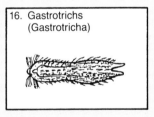

17. Nematodes (Nematoda)

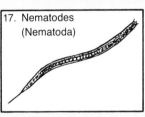

18. Segmented worms (Annelida)

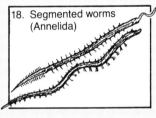

22. Mites (Acarina)

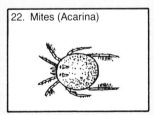

23. Water bears (Tardigrada)

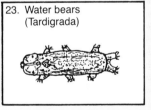

24. Moss animals (Bryozoa)

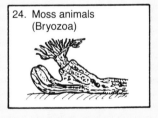

With a little bit of experience, one can then proceed to the subclasses or orders. For instance, the order Zygnematales includes "pond scum" and desmids, and some others that are relatively rare. The class of crustaceans includes Phyllopoda, Copepoda and Ostracoda.

It won't be long until you develop a special interest in one of the groups; one microscopist is fascinated by the desmids, somebody else by the waterfleas. It is very natural to specialize and try to get to know the most important members of your favorite group more intimately.

In the past all this was much more complicated, because information was widely disbursed throughout the literature, and to find it you had to comb through a huge number of publications. I remember also that I could not get any information on algae because I was too young to be admitted to the city library. It was not until I was given a special letter from my biology teacher that the doors of the library were opened to me. I literally had to make drawings at home and then go to a library! Today this is all much easier, as there are inexpensive handbooks and field guides to soil biology, freshwater biology, and marine biology available.

In the following pages, I give a few tips for many basic studies of the microflora and microfauna that may be found in a drop of water.

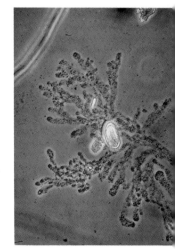

Bacteria (*Zoogloea ramigera*). Photographed by phase contrast method.

Bacteria (Schizomycetes)

High-power magnification (if possible with oil-immersion or phase contrast) is very much recommended for a more detailed examination of these tiny organisms. The very smallest cocci might be at the very limit of your microscope's resolution power. The most easy to observe are the hay bacteria (*Bacillus subtilis*), taken from the growth layer on the surface of a hay infusion. These bacteria line up in typically parallel fashion. They can be distinguished by the shape of their cells: barrel-shaped (cocci), garland-shape chains (*Streptococci*), cubic or in other 3-dimensional packets (*Sarcina*). In addition to the above-mentioned, we also have the rod-shaped cells (bacilli), cells that are shaped like a corkscrew (spirilli), and curved-rod-shaped or rod-shaped cells (Vibrionaceae).

Bacteria also can form long chains and mats that you can see with the naked eye, like the sulfur-containing bacteria *Beggiatoa*. They may be revealed by the color of their coating, like the rust-colored, iron-carrying bacteria found in meadow streams. There are also quite gigantic forms, measuring all of ⅒ mm (.004 in).

Hay bacteria 100× objective (oil-immersion); 8× eyepiece. Top: positive phase contrast. Bottom: negative phase contrast.

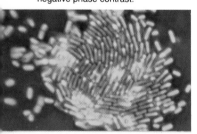

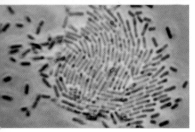

Filamentous blue-green algae of the genus *Oscillatoria*. Low-power magnification and Rheinberg illumination (white light on red background).

Blue-green algae (Cyanobacteria)

Blue-green algae are now classified as eubacteria (true bacteria) and are called *cyanobacteria*. The blue-green algae are grouped as procaryotic organisms, because they do not have a true cell nucleus (the Greek word for nucleus is *karyon*). They are named for their prominent bluish-green color that results from several pigments, diffused throughout the protoplasm. In addition to the typical blue-green color, they can also be recognized by their slimy coating.

They may live in symbiotic association with other organisms, like those of the genus *Nostoc*. Some are motile like those of the genus *Oscillatoria*, which move with jerky motions, the source of their name.

There is a wide variety of blue-green algae, including those that form gelatinous, sometimes chalklike crusts on rocks in mountain streams, fibrous matlike pads on mud-

Blue-green algae (*Nostoc* spec.) filaments in a gelatinous coating. Low-power magnification and blue filter (2 color-conversion filters stacked on top of each other).

died water, and coatings on top of moist soil. The most interesting can be found in very extreme environments, such as heavily polluted waste water and rocky slopes. Another good place to look is on a mill wheel that is periodically immersed in water. Here you can find a very special kind of blue-green algae that form a thick gelatinous coating.

Golden algae (Chrysophyta)

Diatoms

Diatoms (Bacillariophyceae) are the most common and important class of Chrysophyta. They live in freshwater and in saltwater, in varied and often extraordinary forms. Some diatoms have centric (radial) symmetry (order Centrales). They develop a shape like a pillbox, or they hang together in chainlike fibers. They are not motile.

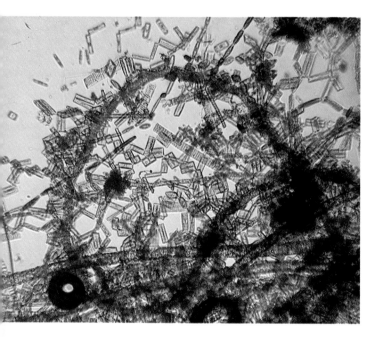

Massive diatom growth on green algae fibers with attached free-moving water forms. The zigzag-shaped *Diatoma vulgare* and the comb-shaped diatoms of the genus *Fragilaria* can be distinguished. Low-power magnification.

The more oblong Pennales, which have a pennate form and bilateral symmetry, and a cleft that stretches the length of the body, called the *raphe*. Cytoplasmic streaming in the raphe is believed to allow the organism to move in caterpillar fashion. This jerky motion, very noticeable in the genus *Navicula*, is recognized by every microscopist.

Diatoms live as free individuals in algae tangles or on mud surfaces. They also form colonies, sitting on gelatinous stems, and cover stones in streams and on lake shores creating a brownish slime layer. The genus *Gomphonema*, which looks like an Egyptian mummy, is abundant.

Some diatoms live in crevices in the soil, an environment where they develop very hard shells. Other, very delicate forms live in freshwater or seawater, like the genera *Asterionella* and *Tabellaria*, whose individual members join to form star-shaped or zigzag forms, respectively, thereby decreasing their sinking speed.

Diatom of the genus *Cymbella*, photographed with simple optics and illumination.

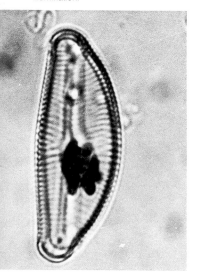

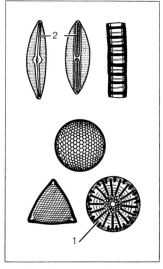

Examples of simple diatoms:
1. Order Centrales (radial symmetry).
2. A pennate, bilaterally symmetric diatom, showing raphe.

Wonderful specimens can be found in Germany in the Lüneburger Heide, and in the U.S. in California, New York, Arizona, and elsewhere. Ocean mud can also contain very beautiful diatom shells. Through a process of washing, followed by heating, the shells can be displayed in their clearest forms. Many microscopists insist that the diatom shells are nature's most beautiful art forms. For instructions on how

Examples of freshwater diatoms:
Left: Phase-contrast photographs.
Above: *Synedra vaucheriae* attached to green algae.
Below: ribbed diatom of the genus *Pinnularia*.

Right: Simple brightfield photographs.
Above: window diatom (*Tabellaria* spec.), beneath it a boat-shaped diatom (*Navicula* spec.) and to its right, a little boat-shaped diatom (*Cymbella* spec.)
Below: star-shaped diatom *Asterionella formosa* and bog diatom (*Fragilaria capucina*).

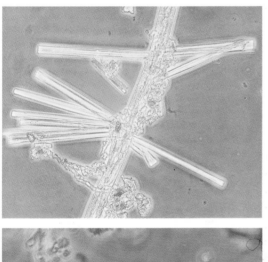

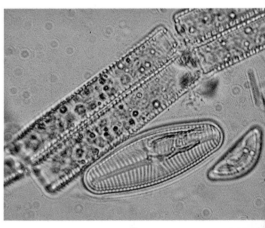

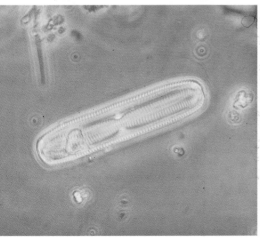

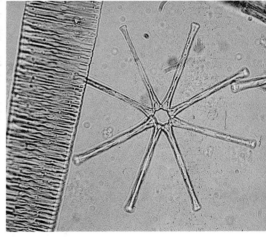

Diatom of the genus *Cymatopleura*. A simple optic and simple illumination (frosted light bulb) reveals only the rough structure of the shell.

to make permanent collections of diatoms, see page 80 to 81.

Since diatom shells, like radiolarian skeletons, almost never deteriorate, their deposits give us much information about earlier life forms. Such microfossils (see page 108) have distinctive, geometrical beauty. Barbados is a famous source of beautiful diatoms.

Golden Algae

A second, less numerous and less well-known class of Chrysophyta is the golden algae (Chrysophyceae). One of the most prevalent species is *Synura uvella*, which may give a brownish color to water. The whorled tree-shapes of the plankton genus *Dinobryon* belongs to this class.

Yellow-Green Algae

The last class of Chrysophyta we will mention are the yellow-green algae (Xanthophyceae), which also produce long fibrous shapes (*Tribonema, Voucheria*).

Green algae (Chlorophyta)

The green algae are one of the most varied groups of organisms found in freshwater. (They are also found in the ocean and on land.) Green algae are eucaryotic protists that have developed into many specialized forms. They vary from simple, independently living, often flagellate forms to groups of cells that in the beginning are small (coccal shapes), to filament-building and tubular shapes. Green algae with flagella can also build colonies. The colonial form might be table-shaped, as in the genus *Gonium*, with 16 cells; mulberry-shaped, as in the genus *Pandorina*, with 32 cells; or ball-shaped, like the *Eudorina*, which also has 32 cells. Some green algae can also form a hollow ball (coenobium), which eventually everts to produce a daughter form; the famous genus *Volvox* is an example.

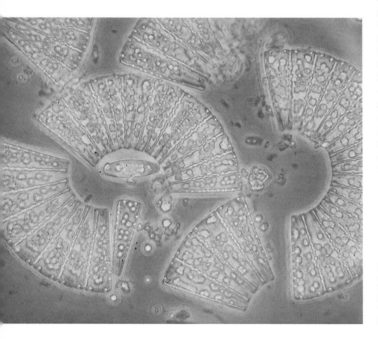

Diatom (*Meridion circulare*), which in spring develops into semicircular bands in meadow streams. It may also form complete circles, but less often. Variable phase-contrast illumination and medium-power magnification.

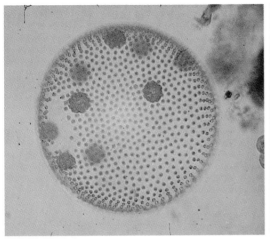

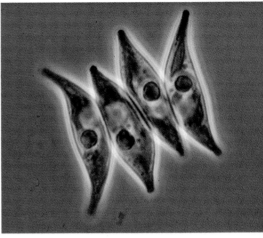

Example of the colony-forming green algae *Volvox aureus*. Each daughter form develops its own colony.

Nonmotile green algae *Scenedesmus acuminatus*. Phase-contrast photography.

Ball-shaped green algae develop together and can consist of either 2 cells (*Euastropsis*), 4 cells (some *Scenedesmus* species), 8 cells (*Scenedesmus bijugatus*), often 16 cells (*Crucigena*), 32 cells (many *Pediastrum* species), and many others. Ball-shaped green algae can be easily identified by their external shape, which sometimes looks remarkably like a piece of jewelry (e.g., *Pediastrum duplex*, which is found in different sizes and also in variable shapes; see photo on page 50).

Green algae of the genus *Scenedesmus*, with or without thorny extensions of greater or lesser length, play an important role in the production of protein from algae cultures. They are the most numerous green algae. Very small, light-

green algae with delicate tips that can live either as individuals or in rodlike bundles (or, when spiral-shaped, in corkscrew fashion) belong to the genus *Ankistrodesmus*.

Green algae can be found anywhere. No garden pond will disappoint you. However, the very smallest of them are often overlooked, like species of the genus *Ankistrodesmus*. Others develop huge stringlike masses, like the member of the genus *Ulothrix* or ones from the genus *Oedogonium* (see photo on page 120).

Zygnemales
Members of this order of filamentous green algae are also

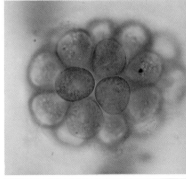

Colony-building green algae: *Eudorina elegans* and *Pandorina morum* (at bottom).

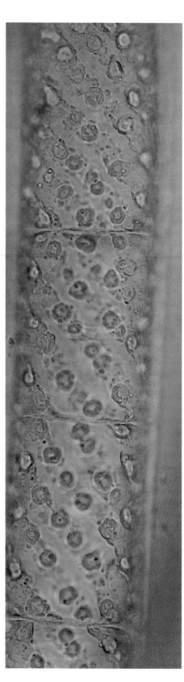

very numerous. Individual filaments hold the chloroplasts in either spiral-shaped bands (e.g., in *Spirogyra*), star-shapes (*Zygnema*), or plates (*Mougeotia*).

During conjugation a "male" and a "female" filament are juxtaposed and communication is established in tubular connections, making the whole look like a ladder. The protoplast from the cell of one filament moves to the filament of the other via these connections. The contents of the cells mixes with those of the other cell, forming a zygote. Algae in the "ladder-forming" stage can always be found in algae mats. With a bit of patience, one can record the exchange of protoplasm from one filament to the other in a series of photos.

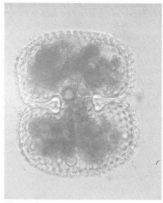

Cosmarium spec, a desmid with lateral indentations.

Filamentous Zygnematales. Far left: *Zygonema* spec. Left: *Spirogyra* spec.

Desmid of the species *Cylindrocystis crassa*, from a peat bog. Kept on a north-facing window in a petri dish, the algae easily survive for one year.

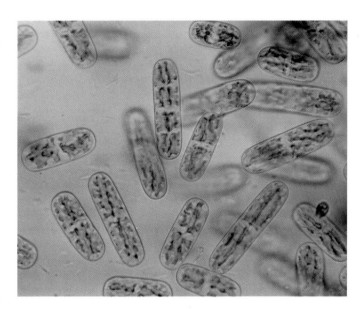

Desmids

Desmids are a much prettier group of green algae; they are enchanting inhabitants that live in places like peat bogs. Squeeze the liquid out of a handful of peat to search for them. Some desmids are filament-shaped; for example, members of the genus *Desmidium* (see photo page 67). Most of them, however, have shapes like small bilaterally symmetric plates that have a deep indentation on each side, like the members of the genera *Cosmarium* and *Micrasterias* (see photos on pages 41 and 67).

The different genera of desmids are easily recognized just by their external shape. Things become more complicated when it comes to recognizing species. For instance, there are many that at first glance look as though they belong to the large genus *Cosmarium*.

The most beautiful forms, like the miniature-star-shaped members of the genus *Micrasterias*, have become very rare, as is the case in general with all tiny organisms living in peat bogs. However, samples taken from peat bogs can be

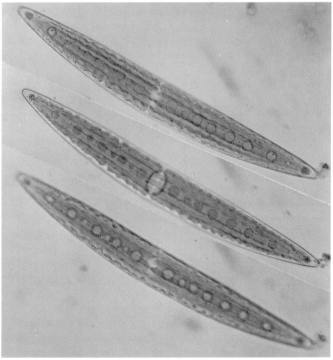

Three photomicrographs of a desmid of the genus *Closterium* at different depths of focus. One can recognize the lobed, green chromatophores.

kept for a long time when they are placed in flat petri dishes that are covered and not exposed to sunlight. I was able to keep the *Cylindrocystis crassa* shown above for a whole year.

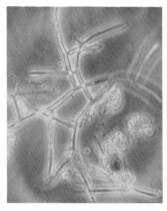

A fungus on a decaying leaf, probably a *Dendrospora erecta*. Phase-contrast photography with red filter.

Fungi

Fungi are a large, diverse group of plantlike organisms that lack chlorophyll and so cannot make their own food. Most fungi live in moist environments. From the few species that live in freshwater, I would recommend *Saprolegnia thureti*, which is found on dead insects and fishes as a cushion-shaped whitish mat. The rigidly extending thread-like filaments (hyphae) end in ball shapes (conidiophores) or may just become wider. They

Amoeba (*Chaos diffluens*). Phase-contrast photography.

contain many flagellated conidia (asexual spores), which are released when the conidiophore breaks.

Zooflagellates (Zoomastigophorea)

Zooflagellates are flagellate protozoa that, in contrast to the plantlike flagellates like *Euglena*, swim in such a way that their flagellae are at the back. They don't perform photosynthesis. When the zooflagellates are firmly attached to a surface, their oscillating flagellae create a suction current that allows food to be swept towards them. In addition to solitary forms, there are colony-building zooflagellates; some are stationary, like *Salpingoeca frequentissima*, which likes to ambush planktonic diatoms.

Amoebas and other Sarcodina

Sarcodina are a subphylum of protozoa that typically move by use of pseudopods.

Naked amoebas (Amoebida)
The amoeba *Hyalodiscus* moves alongside filamentous algae and enters an individual cell, sucking out the contents. The cell contents disappear into the amoeba, which previously was colorless, but now looks green.

Amoebas with long pseudopods are very good species to observe and photograph—for example, *Amoeba hylobates*—because of the way they move. While most of the pseudopods stay still, one pseudopod moves forward and the body flows after it.

Arcellinida
Arcellinida are shelled amoe-

boid protozoans with either lobe-shaped or slender pseudopods. Their shells (tests) may be constructed of several materials. They can be found in freshwater or damp soil. You will be likely to find them when you squeeze out water from a handful of peat, or examine some soil from the edge of a swamp.

Among the most numerous shelled amoeba are those from the genus *Arcella*, which develop a flat, transparent, umbrella-like shell (test). Under high-power magnification, you can see the delicate, honeycombed structure of the test. Members of the genus *Hyalosphenia* have very smooth tests; those of the genus *Euglypha*, and some other genera, have delicate overlapping platelets, arranged like roof tiles. The most conspicuous Arcellinida are from the genus *Difflugia*, whose tests are reinforced by grains of sand, and sometimes even tiny diatom shells. They look like miniature hot-air balloons— sometimes round, sometimes oblong—with one or more points at the end.

Actinopodea

Actinopodea are another group of Sarcodina; they include heliozoans. Sadly, the most interesting heliozoans (e.g., *Actinosphaerium*) are becoming rare. Heliozoans have rodlike, contractile pseudopods called *axopodia*. Tiny organisms stick to the axopodia, and the protoplasm flows inward, carrying its prey with it.

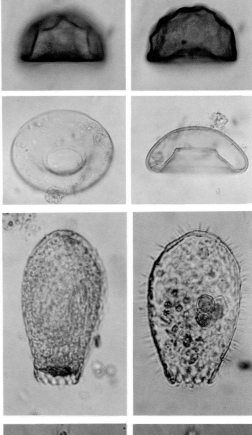

Two photos of *Arcella gibbosa.*

Test of the *Arcella vulgaris;* oblique view and side view.

Tests of an amoeba of the genus *Euglypha.*

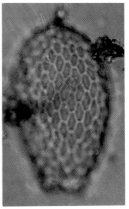

More *Euglypha* tests. Each new focus and method shows different details.

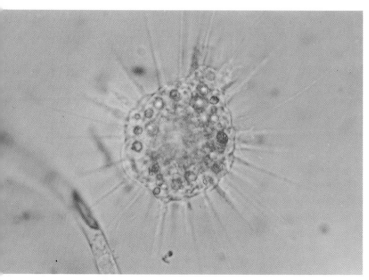

Heliozoan *Actinospherium eichhorni.*

and swims away. In addition to the many species of *Vorticella*, colonies of the freshwater genus *Carchesium* and colonies of *Zoothamnium*, which live on water plants, are also noteworthy. The *Ophrydium versatile*, a gelatinous green spherical species, is unusual. It is often mistaken for green algae that live with the gelatinous ciliates, because individuals share the same gelatinous capsule. The members of the genus *Va-*

The inward movement can easily be observed under dark-field illumination. The heliozoan *Actinophrys sol* is more common than *Actinospherium* and can easily be recognized by its foamy endoplasm.

Ciliates (Ciliophora)

Ciliates are a phylum of protozoa that are among the most advanced unicellular organisms; the variety of shapes they have is immense. The best known is *Paramecium caudatum*, which is easy to culture (see page 120). *Paramecium* belongs to the subclass Nassophoria, which are uniformly covered with cilia, small threadlike appendages that aid in locomotion and feeding.

Movement, food intake and reproduction by conjugation

vary among different species and are an inexhaustible reservoir of possibilities for the action photomicrographer. The *Lacrimaria olor*, for instance, pulls in its long "neck" when swimming. As soon as it becomes stationary, it extends it again and "looks" for food. A ciliate of the genus *Didinium* is a ferocious thief. It will attack a bigger ciliate, penetrate it with a long, rigid proboscis, and suck out its contents.

Ciliates of the groups Peritrichia and Spirotrichea are particularly rewarding subjects for examination. When a peritrich separates from its stalk, it develops a second ring of cilia

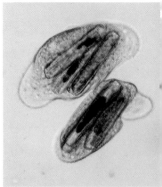

Diatom-eating ciliate (probably *Clidonella*) during and after division. Diatoms almost completely fill the whole interior of the cell.

ginicola live in self-made "cups," either alone or in pairs. The brushlike *Urceolaria* live on flatworms, and members of the genus *Trichodina* attack freshwater polyps and the skin of fish.

The trumpet-shaped ciliates of the genus *Stentor* are well-known. Their bodies are uniformly ciliated. They frequently can be found in aquariums or ponds. The double-lobed, ear-shaped *Folliculina boltoni* lives in a small self-made "bottle."

The Hypotrichia have fused cilia on their underside called *cirri*. Members of the genus *Stylonychia*, and related genera, are noteworthy. You can watch as they "walk" on their cirri on a microscope slide or cover glass. Ciliates of the genus *Euplotes* are smaller and more numerous. All ciliates have cilia at some stage of their lives. Many have rings of cilia, which can be twisted to the left or the right.

Ciliates live in all imaginable biotopes. Particularly rich ciliate fauna can be found in the slimy algae filaments of drainage ditches or in canals that are stone-or cement-lined, where they take up residence. Ciliates play an important role in the food chain of a sewage system's cleansing process.

Ciliates are also considered one of the most important organisms in evaluating water quality. In Germany, for example, Grade I water, "pure or only slightly polluted," is determined by the presence of the

Peritrichous ciliates from the genus *Vorticella*, attached to an algae fiber. Low-power magnification; oblique mixed light.

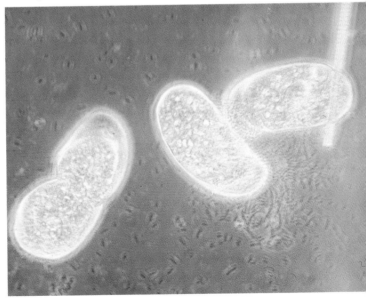

Ciliates of the species *Colpidium colpoda;* the left one is in the process of division. Under phase-contrast illumination, numerous bacteria also are visible.

139

ciliates *Dileptus anser* and *Vorticella similis*. In water of Grade II, moderately polluted water, *Coleps hirtus* live, as well as *Paramecium bursaria*, which contains minute green algae of the genus *Chlorella* (*zoochlorellae*), which live symbiotically in it. In water categorized as Class III, "heavily polluted," many more ciliates live, among others *Lionotus fasciola*, and the well-known *Paramecium caudatum*. In Class IV water, which is even more heavily polluted, there are even more ciliates, among others *Colpidium colpoda* and *Paramecium putrinum*.

The above example of paramecia lets us recognize that closely related species of the same genus can give us an indication of different levels of water quality. However, it is not possible to evaluate water quality simply by establishing the presence of a particular species. That can only be done by studying the whole spectrum of organisms that are present, including bacteria, algae, protozoa, rotatoria, and worms.

Rotifers (Rotatoria)

There is almost no ecological niche in which freshwater rotifers do not exist, and they have developed many forms of nutritional intake.

The huge *wheel organ*, a crown of cilia at the front end, is characteristic. If a rotifer lets go at its hind end, which has an adhesive gland attached to it, the rotating wheel organ propels it forward through the water. If, on the other hand, it decides to stay put, the wheel organ's rotating movement lets it suck in water with food. All you have to do is set up for photography with a shutter speed of 1 second or more and observe a rotifer attached to a surface. The eddies created (under its somewhat depressed position under the cover glass) can be seen beautifully by the rotary movement of the detritus particles, which, under good darkfield illumination, create obvious bright tracks.

Bdelloid (leechlike) rotifers can be found in any mud sample. Their quick, leechlike crawling movements can be easily observed and photographed with flash illumination.

Rotifers that live among plankton, like those of the genus *Brachionus* (which have several different kinds of armor) or those of the genus *Keratella*, can be found regularly when you go "fishing" with a plankton net.

The most beautiful life forms in freshwater are the sessile rotifers. They build themselves shells, from which they reach out with their ciliated lappets to catch prey, for

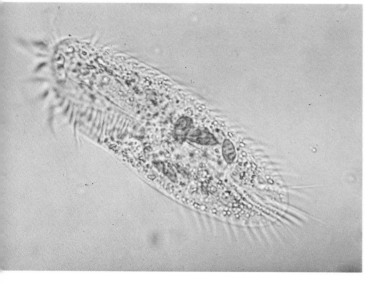

Ciliate *Stylonychia pustulata*.
Brightfield illumination, flash photo.
The smaller organisms of the genus *Euplotes* are somewhat similar in appearance.

example, members of the genus *Floscularia*, which live solitarily on water plants.

Rotifers, particularly the planktonic forms, play a role in the biological food chain that should not be underestimated. There are also those that eat other rotifers, like the large, sacklike members of the genus *Asplanchna*, which eats smaller rotifers that are not protected by long spines.

As is the case with water fleas, rotifers also undergo *seasonal polymorphism*: generations that follow each other during the summer change their absolute size, bodily proportions, the length of the extension of their spines, and so forth. All of these have consequences for their sinking speed and therefore for the way they establish themselves in their environment.

Small rotifers can be smaller than large protozoa, even smaller than ciliates. Nevertheless, they are multicellular. In common with several other groups, they maintain a certain constancy in the number of cells they have. After hatching, they have a specified, predetermined number of cells, which will continue to grow but will not divide.

Water eddies, created by a rotifer of the genus *Brachionus,* were made visible through the presence of particles in the water in darkfield illumination (see text). Exposure time, 1 second.

A split-footed rotifer (*Euchlanis* spec.), photographed with very gentle Rheinberg illumination, with a slight relief effect made by moving the condenser diaphragm a bit to the side.

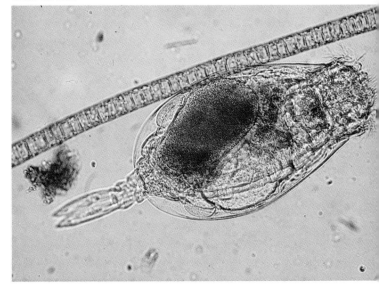

Phyllopoda

Phyllopoda are a class of Crustacea that include tadpole shrimp (Notostraca), clam shrimp (Conchostraca), and water fleas (Cladocera).

There are over 420 species of water fleas. Most are filter feeders. They usually live in plankton-populated areas, and use the leaflike filters (phyllopodia) on their legs to obtain food. Some of them, like *Monospilus dispar*, live in and on the bottom sand and mud.

Others, like the *Chydorus sphaericus*, a true climbing expert, live on the covering of algae filaments. Still others attach themselves to the water surface with their specially shaped shell edges and skim along the underside, like the *Scapholeberis mucronata*. Water fleas also include some predators among their members; they have true legs for catching with real joints, like *Polyphemus pediculus*, which is very conspicuous because of its large eyes, and *Bythotrephes longimanus*, which can grow to almost .4 inch (1 cm), including its caudal spine. Last, but not least, *Leptodora kindtii* can also grow to .4 inch (1 cm), but it is very inconspicuous because it is nearly transparent.

In all, water fleas make highly interesting subjects for observation. They often are very similar, but are well adapted to their particular ecological niches. Those belonging to the species *Daphnia* are quite easy to raise.

Copepods (Copepoda)

Copepods are a diverse order of Crustacea with more than 4,000 species; they only grow to be a few millimeters long. They have very long antennae. Copepods play an important part in the food chain, forming a main component of plankton. For swimming, they use pairs of legs under the thorax in a rowing motion that is carried out with great force, which accounts for their well-

Daphnia longispina, another water flea. Compare the darkfield illumination shown on page 50.

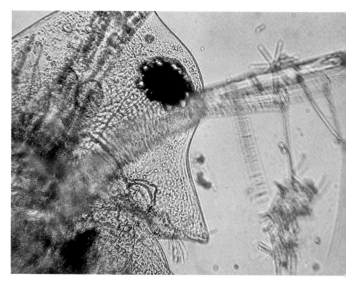

Front end of a water flea (*Leptodora kindtii*). Brightfield–darkfield contrast illumination. The legs are shown at higher magnification on page 55.

First larval stage (nauplius larva) of a copepod. During the time of exposure (1.5 sec.), the animal, initially at rest, moved forward at high speed. Because of its short duration, the jumping phase was not recorded. Phase contrast.

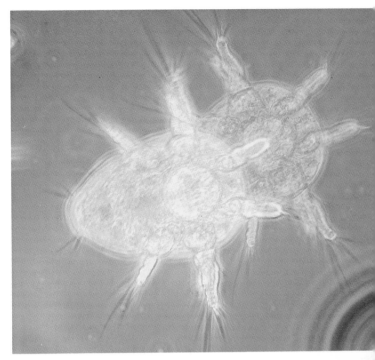

developed leg musculature. (In the photo on the lower right, the leg muscles reflect brightly.) The antennae don't play an essential role in locomotion. With their sudden forward motion, copepods seem to hop inside the water. Copepods can be found in any pond or meadow stream. The females are recognizable by the huge egg sacs that they carry with them all the time, attached to their backs. The abdomen ends in two forked, separated attachments (furca).

In addition to the pond dwellers, there are also larger freshwater forms that are floating species with extraordinarily long antennae; they form part of lake plankton. The females of these species (like those of the genus *Diaptomus*) carry only one single egg pouch. There are also species with shorter antennae, which move more in a crawling fashion along the muddy pond.

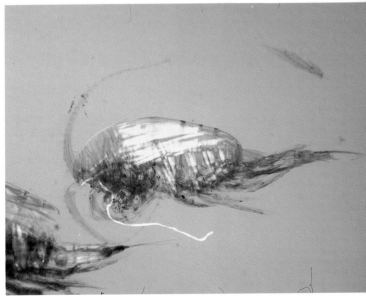

Copepod (*Cyclops* spec.). In polarized light, parts of the trunk and leg muscles reflect brightly.

Seed shrimps (Ostracoda)

Ostracods are another group of minute aquatic Crustacea. The largest ostracods are about ⅛ inch long (3 mm), but usually they are even smaller. Two lateral shell valves surround the organism, which has 7 pairs of appendages and a forked tail (furca). The first two pairs of appendages (antennae) extend outside the shell for locomotion.

Insects (Insecta)

Mature water insects are usually so big that they exceed microorganism size; they don't fit under a cover glass. However, it is possible to find smaller

Young ostracod (*Cyclocypris laevis*). The bristle-covered shell has peritrichous ciliates attached to the outside.

aquatic larval forms as a by-product of a plankton hunt or skimming of the water's surface. The larva of the gnat *Chaoborus plumicornis* is clear as glass. It is just .4 inch (1 cm) long. Only the two pairs of silver-colored swim bladders are noticeable (see photo on the top of the opposite page), which the animal carries inside the thorax and further down, close to the rather conspicuous tail fan.

The larva and pupa of the mosquito are better known—for example, members of the genera *Culex* and *Anopheles*, which make themselves at home in many backyards every summer. The pupae are noticeable for the way they whip their tails to move. Mosquito larvae are tiny, transparent, and wormlike, and continually feed on bacteria, pollen, and sometimes other larvae.

The larvae of the Ceratopogonidae (biting midges) are very thin. They move about like eels, and are found on streams, ponds, and lakes. Fanlike edges with long swim hairs are typical of the legs of the numerous waterbug and water beetle species, like the water beetle on the opposite page (*Haliplus* spec.).

The freshwater microorganisms we have discussed so far should only be considered as samples to stimulate your appetite. Many other fascinating groups of plants and animals could not be even mentioned in this book because of space restrictions. The charts on pages 124–125 and 126–127 give a brief overview of the most important microfauna and microflora groups you are likely to find in freshwater.

The marine microworld

Very briefly, let me touch on what a microscopist can expect at the seashore. In the ocean, many fauna exist in a much greater variety than is the case in freshwater; for instance, the tiny moss animals (bryozoans). Some fauna live only in the ocean: the radiolarians, with their beautiful silicate or strontium sulfate skeletons, and the foraminiferans, with their chalk-strengthened shells. Larvae of echinoderms (starfish, sea urchins, etc.) and many of the numerous species of crustaceans populate plankton; added to these are the Chaetognatha (arrow worms), the Tunicata (tunicates), and others.

Marine organisms may be caught in a plankton net that is dragged behind a boat. Those who snorkel over free-floating mud flats should look for samples of diatoms. Examples of radiolarians, diatoms, and foraminiferans from the ocean are discussed in the chapter on lighting.

Conclusion

We have reached the end of our journey through the microcosmic world, including the delicate structures of plants and animals, a look at the variety of forms of inorganic structures, and the magical world inside a drop of water. More than 90% of all hobby microscopists have undertaken an investigation of the "world in a drop of water." That is no surprise. Microorganisms living in the water have evolved into many different groups with diverse forms, and have adapted to various ecological conditions. Since such microorganisms are easy to observe and are still available in sufficient numbers, they are preferred subjects for the hobby microscopist.

Make your choice; look for a particular area for continued study and deeper understanding. Consult a library for specialized literature in the area you choose. Join a microscopical society; you will meet very interesting people. I hope you have a great deal of fun and much joy with your hobby.

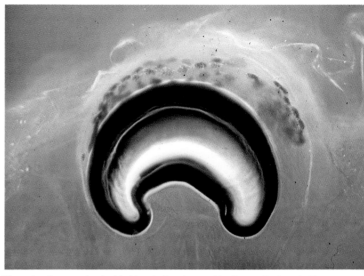

Pigment-cell-covered swim bladder of a larval gnat, *Chaoborus plumicornis*. Two pairs of swim bladders keep the larva, which is about ⅜-inch long (1 cm) floating horizontally in the water.

Swimming adaptations of a water beetle (*Haliplus* spec.), flattened legs and a thick layer of swimming hair. Rheinberg illumination with a noticeable central field.

145

APPENDIXES

Microscopy with children and adolescents

Children are much better able to absorb information than we think they are. I have seen 5-year-olds looking through a microscope, absolutely spellbound, if I provided the technique for them. Who knows? Perhaps the "little animals running around in a drop of water" or a beautiful diatom or desmid is going to be the trig-

distance between our eyes (interpupillary distance), and set the binocular adjustment of the inspection microscope accordingly. The room is slightly darkened. The next step is focusing: the little hand—in the beginning guided by a big hand—begins to turn the coarse adjustment knob to focus. It is not difficult to catch the child's attention for one or two minutes and, of course, curiosity makes her ask, what is all of this and where is it coming from?

things to her in playful fashion, but the interest faded away rather quickly, since she could not hold everything in her hands.

As a hobby microscopist, I always encourage children to take a look through the microscope (a stereomicroscope is a must), but I always am sparing with explanations. A microscope is a wonderful instrument to awaken curiosity about the unknown, and children are known to ask questions that quickly get to the limit of even our knowledge.

As far as the choice of subjects is concerned: for children, use what appeals to them; for young people, whatever they are interested in. It is best to start with something totally concrete, like a little flower that they can take home with them. Put a bit of pollen under the microscope and let them look at it under medium-power magnification. Pollen disburses in tiny little balloon shapes, and you can explain that these little things do actually float because of delicate movements in the air, just as balloons do.

Of course, the famous "world in a drop of water" also gives us many suitable subjects. Water blooms are best. Why did the garden pond all of a sudden turn green? A small drop on a glass slide will display many flagellates, busily moving about.

Small insects, viewed either with low-power magnification or binocular enlargements, are also good subjects. You should refrain from mounting por-

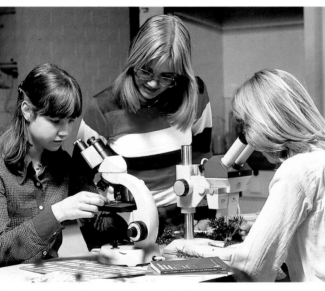

Microscopy can be a lively leisure-time activity for teenagers.

ger that will make them sensitive towards life and instill in them a sense of beauty.

First, I sit my little guest down on a chair that has good padding so that he or she won't tire easily. Next, we take a piece of paper and two marker pens and measure the

When my little daughter was still in elementary school, she would always come by in the evening to watch me when I experimented with my microscope. The diatom "boats," moving with jerky motions, were her particular favorites. I was able to explain many

tions of insects, like the head or legs. Rather, gently attach the whole insect to the slide, using the beeswax foot method (p. 122), so that it is still possible to move its legs, but it will not get injured.

Cross-sections of plants and, of course, of animals are less suitable. If you talk about "cutting," the child will react negatively. Such studies should not be undertaken until the child is 8 or 9 years old.

Children go through distinct developmental stages during which they paint symmetrical, colorful figures or fold paper into symmetrical shapes. This is an excellent time to show symmetrical diatoms and cross-sections of grass stems, as examples of the symmetrical beauty in nature. A cross-section of the spine of a sea urchin also may stimulate a sense of form and color.

Of particular interest for young viewers, in my experience, are those microscopic images with a moving subject, as long as the movements are not too fast. A slowly moving amoeba, or a heliozoan that shows the flow of cytoplasm in its pseudopods, will do well, as will ciliates. They move much more slowly when the water in the preparation is slightly stale, and one can observe them as they congregate at the edges of the cover glass, where more oxygen is available to them.

You can also try to stimulate a sense of spatial relationships in young people by showing them developmental slides of something—for instance, the tooth development shown on page 68. When the microscopist patiently explains the process, young people will get an idea of how such structures develop, harden over time, how enamel develops, and so forth. Specimens can also be viewed and discussed from a functional point of view. For instance, with a picture of star-shaped cells, it's possible to understand how the parts of a rush support each other; a similar idea can be learned from bone development.

Another source of interest for young people, from the age of about 12 years on, are samples taken from their own bodies. Young people still remember when one of their deciduous teeth fell out: let them look at a slide that shows tooth development. If a child has had an accident and has lost a fingernail or toenail, show him or her a cross-section of the nail bed. If a young man is starting to shave, a skin sample can show the development of hair. Everything that a young person has experienced himself or herself generates interest and encourages curiosity. When he or she looks at a slide that "accidentally" deals with a subject that relates to personal experience, understanding is deepened automatically.

If you have children of your own, wait and see what kind of relationship they might develop to dad's or mom's microscopy hobby. If they show interest, give them a simple but sturdy microscope for Christmas to which accessories can be added later on. Nothing will replace having one's own equipment. Of course, don't set your expectations too high: competition for their time is fierce. I was able to give many young people insight into the world of microscopy, particularly when I was a student involved in making many of the accessories myself, living in a small village, having all kinds of time to pursue my interest. Even though only one friend stayed with it and made microscopy his hobby, I know that many others still know where to find desmids and what *Micrasterias* looks like. This probably is not very useful in relationship to their work, but the sense that there is a whole other world "out there" in addition to their own has made a difference in their lives.

To meet fellow enthusiasts, do not hesitate to advertise your hobby. Motorcycle clubs, model airplane clubs, dance clubs, and choral societies do it all the time. Every one of these clubs needs young people. Even microscopists, whether they work alone or are members of an organization, should not be shy; so be assertive.

147

LIST OF SUPPLIERS

Microscope manufacturers/representatives in the United States and other English-speaking countries:

Accu-Scope, Inc.
8 Roslyn Drive
Glen Head, N.Y. 11545
USA
tel. (516) 759-1000
fax (516) 674-3309

Carl Zeiss, Inc.
Microscope Division
One Zeiss Drive
Thornwood, New York 10594
USA
tel. (800) 233-2343
fax (914) 681-7445

Carl Zeiss (Oberkochen) Ltd.
17–20 Woodfield Road
Welwyn Garden City
Herts AL7 ILU
United Kingdom

Carl Zeiss Canada
Microscope Division
45 Valleybrook Drive
Don Mills, Ontario M3B 2S6
Canada

Carl Zeiss Pty., Ltd.
114 Pyrmont Bridge Road
Camperdown, N.S.W. 2050
Australia

Carl Zeiss (New Zealand) Ltd.
Four Seasons Plaza
22 Emily Place
Auckland 1
New Zealand

Eschenbach Optik of America
904 Ethan Allen Highway
Ridgefield, CT 06877
USA
tel. (203) 438-7471
fax (203) 231-4718

(Eschenbach in UK)
Associated Optical Products
Unit 2 Eton Place
64 High Street
Burnham, Buckinghamshire
SL1 7JT, Great Britain

(Eschenbach in Canada)
Science Import
PO Box 47030
Sillery, Quebec
G1S 4X1 Canada

(Eschenbach in New Zealand)
Optical Enterprises Ltd.
Arthur Cocks and Company
PO Box 750
Auckland 1, New Zealand

(Euromex in U.K.)
Meta Scientific Ltd.
7 Fosters Grove
Windlesham, Surrey
GU 20 6JZ
United Kingdom
tel. 0276-47-54-07
fax 0276-47-20-70

and

NES Arnold Ltd.
Ludlow Hill Rd.
West Bridgford
Nottingham NG 2 6 HD
United Kingdom

[Note: some Hund microscopes are distributed in the United States by:
Seiler Instrument and Manufacturing
Company
170 East Kirkham Avenue
St. Louis, MO 63119-1791
tel. (314) 968-2282
fax (314) 968-2637]

Leica
111 Deer Lake Road
Deerfield, Illinois 60015
USA
tel. (708) 405-0123
fax (708) 405-0147

Leica Canada, Inc.
513 McNicoll Ave.
Willowdale, Ontario
M2H 2C9 Canada
tel. (416) 497-2460
fax (416) 497-2053

Leica UK Ltd.
Davy Avenue
Knowlhill
Milton Keynes
MK5 8LB
United Kingdom
tel. 44-908-666-663
fax 44-908-609-992

Leica Instruments Pty. Ltd.
45 Epping Road
PO Box 21
North Ryde, NSW 2113
Australia
tel. 61-2-888-7122
fax 61-2-888-7526

Olympus America Inc.
(for U.S. and Canada)
Precision Instrument Division
4 Nevada Drive
Lake Success, NY 11042-1179
USA
tel. (718) 895-0843
fax (516) 222-7920

[Note: some PZO microscopes and parts
are distributed in the United States by:
TCI Tyrolit Co., Inc.
367 Route 109
West Babylon, New York 11704
USA
tel. (516) 422-2000
fax (516) 661-6798]

Swift Instruments, Inc.
PO Box 562
San José, California 95106
USA
tel. (408) 292-2380
fax (408) 292-7967

Swift Instruments in UK:
Pyser-SGI, Ltd.
Fircroft Way
Edinbridge, Kent
United Kingdom TN8 6HA
fax 44-732-865-544
tel. 44-762-864-111

Swift Instruments in rest of world:

Swift Instruments, Int.
Nakano 6-22-10
Nakano-Ku, Tokyo
Japan 164
fax (03) 3362-4488
tel. (03) 3362-4400

Swift Instruments in Canada

VWR Scientific/Sargent-Welch
77 Enterprise Drive North
London, Ontario N6N 1A5
Canada
fax (519) 649-5444
tel. (519) 649-5454

Vickers Instruments
Haxby Road
York YO3 YSD England
United Kingdom

Manufacturers of microscopes in Germany and other parts of Europe that should be contacted directly:

Askania-Werke Rathenow
Geschwister-Scholl-Str. 10/11
14712 Rathenow, Germany
tel. 011-49-3385-8900
fax 011-49-3385-2403

Euromex*
Papenkamp 20 Rijkerswaerd
6836 BD Arnhem, Holland
tel. 011-31-85-234124
fax 011-31-85-232833

Franckh–Kosmos-Verlagsgesellschaft
Pfizerstraße 5-7
70184 Stuttgart, Germany
tel. 011-49-711-21910

Hertel & Reuss
Quellhofstraße 67
34127 Kassel, Germany
tel. 011-49-561-83006
fax 011-49-561-893308

R. Göke
Bahnhofstraße 27
58095 Hagen, Germany

Helmut Hund GmbH*
Wetzlaren Str. 145
35580 Wetzlar–Nauborn, Germany
tel. 011-49-6441-20040
fax 011-49-6441-200444

Microthek, GmbH
Blücherstraße 11
22727 Hamburg, Germany
tel. 011-49-40-381536
fax 011-49-40-381538

Nachet
106 Rue Chaptal
1192306 Levallois-Peret
France

Neckermann Versand AG
Hanauer Landstr. 360
60386 Frankfurt, Germany
tel. 011-49-69-40401
fax 011-49-69-419078

PZO (Polskie Zaklady Optyczne)*
% Labimex, Ltd.
Spólka Handlu Zaglanicznego
(Foreign Trade Company, Ltd.)
ul. Krakowskie Przedmieście 79
00-079 Warsaw, Poland
fax 48-22-6356347

Quelle Schickedanz AG & Co.
Nurnburger Str. 91-95
90762 Fürth, Germany
tel. 011-49-911-140
fax 011-49-911-708580

Arthur Siebert Wetzlar GmbH
(EMO)
Optik u. Feinmechanik
Frankenstrasse 2
35578 Wetzlar, Germany
tel. 011-49-6441-22735

---

*See page 148 and 149 also.

INDEX

METRIC EQUIVALENTS AND OTHER USEFUL UNITS

1 cm = .0394 inch
1 inch = 2.54 cm
1 liter = 33.8 fluid oz.
1 fluid oz. = 0.03 liter
1 cm^3 = 1 mL (milliliter) = .061 $in.^3$
1 mL = 1 milliliter = 1/1000 liter
1 μm = 1 micrometer = 1/1 000 000 meter or 1×10^{-6} meter
1 nm = 1 nanometer = 1/1 000 000 000 meter or 1×10^{-9} meter

Photo and Illustration Credits:
Accu-Scope: 18, middle row, left
Emo: 19
Eschenbach Optik GmbH: 21
Fischer-Verlag: 86, 92
Göke: 105
A. Hauck: 41, bottom
Hertel and Reuss: 18, middle row, right; 73, 43 top
Helmut Hundt GmbH (formerly Wills): 56 bottom
Kosmos-Verlagsgesellschaft: 113, top
Leica AG (formerly E. Leitz): 31; 33; 57, bottom right
Leica AG (formerly C. Reichert): 17
Leica Inc. Optical Products Division, Buffalo, New York, 18, middle row, center
Leica (formerly Wild-Heerbrugg): 75; 115, left
Lieder: 74, bottom; 130, bottom right
Microthek (formerly Jungner): 13; 18 top row, center; 101; 121, top
Olympus 12; 18 (courtesy of Olympus America) bottom, left; 28; 61; 75, left
PZO (Göke) 18, top, left; 30, bottom; 59, 60, 105, 108, 121, top
Swift: 18, top right; 20, top
Carl Zeiss: 6 left; 6 bottom; 18, bottom right; 29; 30, top; 43, bottom; 56, top; 64, top.
Photo page 41 top: after W. W. Frank, revised
Drawing page 44: a copy from Wild-Heerbrugg
Drawings pp. 77 top, 93 below, 121 middle, 121 below, 122: K. Hanitzsch
Drawing p. 74 top right: B. Kresling
Drawing on p. 130 from Meyer and Lieder, *Begleitbuch zu Mikroskopischen Präparaten und Microdias.* J. Lieder, Ludwigsburg, 1984.
All other photos and drawings are those of the author